Contents

Death-by-Chocolate Cake

MAKES 1 (9-INCH) TWO-LAYER FROSTED CAKE

Prep time: 35 minutes

 Cook time: 28 minutes

Ingredients:

FOR THE CAKE

- Shortening, for preparing the pans
- 157 grams All-Purpose Flour Blend , plus more for dusting
- 75 grams unsweetened natural cocoa powder
- 62 grams arrowroot
- 2 teaspoons ground espresso
- 2 teaspoons baking soda
- 1 teaspoon baking powder
- 1 teaspoon xanthan gum
- 1 teaspoon salt
- 350 grams cane sugar or granulated sugar
- 1 cup avocado oil or canola oil
- 2 large eggs
- 1 cup whole milk or coconut milk beverage
- 60 grams vanilla Greek yogurt or nondairy alternative
- 1 shot brewed espresso, cooled (optional)
- 2 tablespoons vanilla extract
- 1 teaspoon apple cider vinegar

FOR THE CHOCOLATE BUTTERCREAM FROSTING

- 136 grams shortening
- 720 grams powdered sugar
- 75 grams unsweetened natural cocoa powder
- 2 teaspoons vanilla extract
- 6 tablespoons whole milk or coconut milk beverage

Directions:

TO MAKE THE CAKE

Step 1

Preheat the oven to 350°F. Grease two 9-inch springform pans with shortening. Sprinkle a little flour inside and tap the pans to spread the flour evenly around each pan.

Step 2

In a medium bowl, whisk the flour, cocoa powder, arrowroot, ground espresso, baking soda, baking powder, xanthan gum, and salt to combine.

Step 3

In a large bowl, using a whisk or handheld electric mixer, beat the sugar, oil, eggs, milk, yogurt, brewed espresso (if using), vanilla, and vinegar until well mixed, stopping to scrape down the bowl as needed. Slowly add the flour mixture and mix until combined.

Step 4

Evenly divide the batter between the prepared pans.

Step 5

Bake for 25 to 28 minutes, or until a toothpick inserted into the center of a cake comes out clean.

Step 6

Let the cakes cool in the pans for at least 15 minutes. Release the clamp from each pan and remove the sides. Transfer the cakes and plates to a wire rack to cool completely.

Step 7

Using a large serrated knife, cut off the thin domed layer from the top of each cake. Creating a flat surface will help the cakes stack well.

TO MAKE THE CHOCOLATE BUTTERCREAM FROSTING

Step 8

In a large bowl, using a handheld electric mixer, beat the shortening until smooth and creamy. Add the powdered sugar, cocoa powder, and vanilla. Mix, while slowly adding the milk, until smooth and creamy.

Step 9

Frost the cake layers and outside of the cake as desired. Refrigerate leftovers, covered, for up to 5 days.

Super Moist Cream Cheese Pound Cake

MAKES 1 TUBE CAKE
Prep time: 20 minutes
 Cook time: 1 hour 20 minutes

Ingredients:

* Shortening, for preparing the pan

* 375 grams All-Purpose Flour Blend

* 3 tablespoons arrowroot
* 1 teaspoon xanthan gum
* ½ teaspoon baking powder
* ¼ teaspoon salt

- 24 tablespoons (3 sticks) butter or nondairy alternative
- 1 (8-ounce) package cream cheese or nondairy alternative
- 500 grams cane sugar or granulated sugar
- 80 grams vanilla Greek yogurt or nondairy alternative
- 6 large eggs, beaten
- 2 teaspoons vanilla extract

Directions:

Step 1

Preheat the oven to 325°F. Grease a 10- to 12-cup Bundt pan with shortening.

Step 2

In a medium bowl, whisk the flour, arrowroot, xanthan gum, baking powder, and salt to combine.

Step 3

In a large bowl, using a handheld electric mixer on medium speed, cream together the butter and cream cheese, stopping to scrape down the bowl as needed. Add the sugar and mix well. Add the yogurt, beaten eggs, and vanilla. Mix until combined.

Step 4

Add the flour mixture to the wet ingredients and mix just until combined. Do not overmix.

Step 5

Pour the batter into the prepared Bundt pan and tap the pan on the counter to remove any air bubbles.

Step 6

Bake for 1 hour 15 minutes to 1 hour 20 minutes, or until a toothpick inserted into the center of the pound cake comes out clean.

Step 7

Let the cake cool completely in the pan. This may take 1 to 2 hours. Invert the cake over a wire rack and remove it from the pan. Keep covered at room temperature, or refrigerate, for up to 5 days.

Angel Food Cake

MAKES 1 (10-INCH) CAKE

Prep time: 25 minutes

Cook time: about 1 hour

Ingredients:

- 156 grams All-Purpose Flour Blend
- 350 grams cane sugar or granulated sugar
- 2 tablespoons arrowroot

- ½ teaspoon xanthan gum
- ¼ teaspoon salt
- 1½ cups egg whites (about 12 large eggs; see Tip)
- 1 teaspoon cream of tartar
- ½ teaspoon vanilla extract
- ½ teaspoon orange extract

Directions:

Step 1

Position an oven rack to the third lowest position and preheat the oven to 325°F.

Step 2

In a food processor, combine the flour, sugar, arrowroot, xanthan gum, and salt. Process to a fine powdery texture.

Step 3

In a large bowl, using a handheld electric mixer, beat the egg whites until they form stiff peaks. Be careful not to overmix. Add the cream of tartar, vanilla, and orange extract and give a quick stir with a spatula.

Step 4

Using the spatula, fold the flour mixture into the egg whites. Do not overmix.

Step 5

Pour the batter into an ungreased 10-inch tube pan.

Step 6

Bake for 50 to 60 minutes, or until a toothpick inserted into the center of the cake comes out clean.

Step 7

On a wire rack, invert the cake and let it cool in the pan. When completely cooled, remove the cake from the pan. Keep leftovers covered at room temperature for up to 3 days, or refrigerate for up to 5 days.

Carrot Cake

MAKES 1 (9-INCH) TWO-LAYER FROSTED CAKE

Prep time: 30 minutes

Cook time: about 35 minutes

Ingredients:

FOR THE CAKE

- Shortening, for preparing the pan
- 250 grams All-Purpose Flour Blend , plus more for dusting
- 62 grams arrowroot

- 2 teaspoons baking powder
- 2 teaspoons ground cinnamon
- 1 teaspoon xanthan gum
- 1 teaspoon baking soda
- 1 teaspoon ground ginger
- ½ teaspoon salt
- ¼ teaspoon ground nutmeg
- ¼ teaspoon ground cloves
- 300 grams light brown sugar
- 100 grams cane sugar or granulated sugar
- 1 cup avocado oil or canola oil
- 4 large eggs
- 180 grams unsweetened applesauce
- 1 teaspoon vanilla extract
- 1 teaspoon apple cider vinegar
- 220 grams grated carrot (about 6 small carrots)
- 55 grams canned crushed pineapple, drained (optional)
- 50 grams shredded coconut (optional)
- 62 grams chopped nuts (optional)

FOR THE CREAM CHEESE FROSTING

- 2 (8-ounce) packages cream cheese or nondairy alternative
- 8 tablespoons (1 stick) butter or nondairy alternative
- 2 to 3 tablespoons whole milk or coconut milk beverage
- 1 teaspoon vanilla extract
- ⅛ teaspoon salt
- 720 grams powdered sugar

Directions:

TO MAKE THE CAKE

Step 1

Preheat the oven to 350°F. Grease two 9-inch springform pans with shortening. Sprinkle a little flour inside and tap the pans to spread the flour evenly around each pan.

Step 2

In a medium bowl, whisk the flour, arrowroot, baking powder, cinnamon, xanthan gum, baking soda, ginger, salt, nutmeg, and cloves to combine.

Step 3

In a large bowl, using a whisk or handheld electric mixer, beat together the brown sugar, cane sugar, oil, eggs, applesauce, vanilla, and vinegar until combined, making sure there are no clumps of brown sugar remaining.

Step 4

Using a spatula, fold the flour mixture into the wet ingredients in two parts, mixing between each. Fold until just combined. Gently fold in the carrots. If using, fold in the pineapple, coconut, and nuts.

Step 5

Evenly divide the batter between the prepared cake pans.

Step 6

Bake for 30 to 35 minutes, or until a toothpick inserted in the center of a cake comes out clean.

Step 7

Let the cakes cool in the pans for 15 minutes. Release the clamp from each pan and remove the sides. Transfer the cakes and plates to a wire rack to cool completely.

TO MAKE THE CREAM CHEESE FROSTING

Step 8

In a large bowl, using a handheld electric mixer on medium speed, cream together the cream cheese and butter until smooth.

Step 9

Reduce the speed to low and add the milk, vanilla, salt, and powdered sugar. Mix until smooth and creamy.

Step 10

Frost the cake as desired. Refrigerate leftovers, covered, for up to 4 days.

Gooey Butter Cake

MAKES 1 (9-BY-13-INCH) CAKE
Prep time: 15 minutes
 Cook time: about 45 minutes

Ingredients:

FOR THE BOTTOM CAKE LAYER

- Shortening, for preparing the pan

- 250 grams All-Purpose Flour Blend

- 150 grams cane sugar or granulated sugar
- 1 tablespoon baking powder
- 1 teaspoon xanthan gum
- 8 tablespoons (1 stick) butter or nondairy alternative, melted
- 2 large eggs
- 1 teaspoon vanilla extract

FOR THE TOP CREAMY LAYER

- 1 (8-ounce) package cream cheese or nondairy alternative
- 2 large eggs
- 1 teaspoon vanilla extract
- 480 grams powdered sugar

Directions:

TO MAKE THE BOTTOM CAKE LAYER

Step 1

Preheat the oven to 350°F. Grease a 9-by-13-inch pan with shortening.

Step 2

In a medium bowl, whisk the flour, sugar, baking powder, and xanthan gum to combine. Add the melted butter, eggs, and vanilla. Using a spatula, stir to combine.

Step 3

Using your clean hands, continue to mix, forming a dough. Press it firmly into the prepared pan.

TO MAKE THE TOP CREAMY LAYER

Step 4

In a large bowl, using a handheld electric mixer, beat the cream cheese until smooth. Add the eggs and vanilla. Mix for 2 minutes until well combined.

Step 5

With the mixer on low speed, slowly add the powdered sugar, 120 grams (1 cup) at a time. Mix until a batter forms. Pour the batter over the bottom layer.

Step 6

Bake for 40 to 45 minutes, or until the top becomes golden.

Step 7

Let the cake cool before slicing. Refrigerate leftovers, covered, for up to 1 week.

Lemon Lover's Bundt Cake

MAKES 1 BUNDT CAKE

Prep time: 45 minutes

 Cook time: 50 minutes

Ingredients:

FOR THE CAKE

- Shortening, for preparing the pan

- 375 grams All-Purpose Flour Blend

- 1 teaspoon xanthan gum
- 1 teaspoon salt
- ½ teaspoon baking powder
- ½ teaspoon baking soda
- 16 tablespoons (2 sticks) butter or nondairy alternative
- 400 grams cane sugar or granulated sugar
- 4 large eggs
- ½ teaspoon vanilla extract
- 30 grams grated lemon zest (about 8 lemons)
- ½ cup fresh lemon juice (about 4 lemons)
- 1 cup buttermilk, or 1 cup coconut milk beverage plus 1 tablespoon apple cider vinegar (see here)

FOR THE LEMON SYRUP

- 100 grams cane sugar or granulated sugar
- ½ cup fresh lemon juice (about 4 lemons)

FOR THE GLAZE

- 120 grams powdered sugar
- 2 tablespoons whole milk or coconut milk beverage
- ¼ teaspoon vanilla extract
- ¼ teaspoon lemon extract

Directions:

TO MAKE THE CAKE

Step 1

Preheat the oven to 350°F. Grease a 10- to 12-cup Bundt pan with shortening.

Step 2

In a medium bowl, whisk the flour, xanthan gum, salt, baking powder, and baking soda to combine.

Step 3

In a small bowl, using a handheld electric mixer on medium speed, cream together the butter and sugar.

Step 4

In a third bowl, whisk the eggs, vanilla, lemon zest, and lemon juice to blend. Add this to the creamed butter and sugar. Mix well to combine. It will look curdled, but that's okay.

Step 5

Add half the flour mixture and ½ cup of buttermilk to the egg mixture and mix on low speed to blend. Add the remaining ½ cup of buttermilk and then the remaining flour mixture and mix just until everything is combined. Do not overmix.

Step 6

Pour the batter into the prepared Bundt pan.

Step 7

Bake for 40 to 45 minutes, or until a toothpick inserted into the center of the cake comes out clean.

Step 8

Let the cake cool in the pan for 15 minutes while you prepare the lemon syrup.

TO MAKE THE LEMON SYRUP

Step 9

In a small saucepan, combine the sugar and lemon juice. Cook over medium heat, stirring, until the sugar is completely dissolved. Bring the syrup to a boil and boil for 2 to 3 minutes. Remove from the heat and let the syrup cool. It will thicken a little as it cools.

Step 10

Line a baking sheet with parchment paper and set a wire rack in the pan. Remove the cake from the Bundt pan and flip it over onto the wire rack. Slowly pour the cooled syrup over the cake and allow the cake to soak it up.

Step 11

Let the cake cool completely.

TO MAKE THE GLAZE

Step 12

In a small bowl, whisk the powdered sugar, milk, vanilla, and lemon extract until smooth. Drizzle the glaze over the cake top and serve.

Step 13

Keep covered at room temperature, or refrigerate, for up to 5 days.

Classic Cheesecake

MAKES 1 (9-INCH) CHEESECAKE
Prep time: 1 hour
 Cook time: about 3 hours, plus overnight chilling

Ingredients:

FOR THE CRUST

- 95 grams All-Purpose Flour Blend , plus more for dusting

- ¼ teaspoon xanthan gum
- ¼ teaspoon salt
- 8 tablespoons (1 stick) butter or nondairy alternative
- 50 grams cane sugar or granulated sugar
- 1 large egg yolk
- 1 teaspoon vanilla extract

FOR THE CHEESECAKE FILLING

- 4 (8-ounce) packages cream cheese or nondairy alternative, room temperature
- 300 grams cane sugar or granulated sugar
- 80 grams vanilla Greek yogurt or nondairy alternative
- 1 tablespoon vanilla extract
- 2 large egg yolks
- 4 large eggs

Directions:

TO MAKE THE CRUST

Step 1

Line the bottom of a 9-inch springform pan with aluminum foil and dust with a bit of flour. The foil should wrap around the entire bottom portion of the pan, including the outside.

Step 2

In a small bowl, whisk the flour, xanthan gum, and salt to combine.

Step 3

In a large bowl, using a whisk or handheld electric mixer, mix the butter, sugar, egg yolk, and vanilla until combined. Add the flour mixture and mix until a sticky dough forms.

Step 4

Transfer the dough to the prepared pan and dust a bit more flour on top so it doesn't stick to your fingers. Flatten the dough into a 6-inch-diameter disk, cover with plastic wrap, and chill for 30 minutes.

Step 5

Position an oven rack in the third lowest position and preheat the oven to 350°F.

Step 6

Release the clamp from the pan and remove the sides. Place a small piece of parchment paper over the chilled dough and use a rolling pin to stretch the dough to reach the edges of the pan. Work the edges so the dough fits well. Replace the sides of the pan, and tighten the clamp. Use your fingertips to push the dough up the sides just a little.

Step 7

Bake for 10 minutes. Remove from the oven but leave the oven on. Leave the oven rack where it is, but increase the oven temperature to 500°F.

Step 8

Let the crust cool for at least 10 minutes before preparing the cheesecake filling.

TO MAKE THE CHEESECAKE FILLING

Step 9

In a large bowl, using a whisk or handheld electric mixer, beat the cream cheese until smooth and creamy. Add the sugar, yogurt, and vanilla and mix again to combine. Add the egg yolks only and mix again.

Step 10

Add the whole eggs, 2 at a time, mixing after each set and stopping to scrape down the bowl as needed, also giving the bottom of the bowl a stir to make sure all the cream cheese is incorporated. Pour the batter over the cooled crust.

Step 11

Bake for 10 minutes, then (without opening the oven) reduce the oven temperature to 200°F and bake for 2 hours 30 minutes. The edges will be golden but the center may not be quite set. If you have an instant-read thermometer, the internal temperature should read 165°F.

Step 12

Let the cake sit in the pan at room temperature for 2 hours. Cover it with plastic wrap and refrigerate overnight.

Step 13

To remove the cake from the pan, run a butter knife along the outside of the cake to detach it from the sides. Release the clamp and remove the sides. Refrigerate, covered, for up to 4 days.

Triple-Layer Birthday Cake with Buttercream Frosting

MAKES 1 (9-INCH) THREE-LAYER FROSTED CAKE

Prep time: 30 minutes
 Cook time: 30 minutes

Ingredients:

FOR THE CAKE

- Shortening, for preparing the pans
- 375 grams All-Purpose Flour Blend , plus more for dusting
- 62 grams arrowroot
- 1 tablespoon baking powder
- 1½ teaspoons xanthan gum
- 1 teaspoon baking soda
- ½ teaspoon salt
- 3 large eggs

- 2 large egg whites
- 400 grams cane sugar or granulated sugar
- 1½ cups whole milk or coconut milk beverage
- 1 cup avocado oil or canola oil
- 1 tablespoon vanilla extract
- 1 teaspoon apple cider vinegar

FOR THE BUTTERCREAM FROSTING

- 205 grams shortening
- 8 tablespoons (1 stick) butter or nondairy alternative
- 720 grams powdered sugar
- 2 teaspoons vanilla extract
- ¼ cup heavy cream or coconut cream

Directions:

TO MAKE THE CAKE

Step 1

Preheat the oven to 350°F. Grease three 9-inch springform pans with shortening. Sprinkle a little flour inside and tap the pans to spread the flour evenly around each pan.

Step 2

In a medium bowl, whisk the flour, arrowroot, baking powder, xanthan gum, baking soda, and salt to combine.

Step 3

In a small bowl, whisk the whole eggs to combine.

Step 4

In a large bowl, using a handheld electric mixer, whip the egg whites until soft peak forms. Add the cane sugar and beaten eggs to the egg whites and mix for 1 minute.

Step 5

Add the milk, oil, vanilla, and vinegar. Mix well. With the mixer on low speed, mix in the flour in 3 additions, stopping to scrape down the bowl, as needed.

Step 6

Evenly divide the batter between the prepared pans.

Step 7

Bake for 25 to 30 minutes, or until a toothpick inserted into the center of a cake comes out clean.

Step 8

Let the cakes cool in the pans for at least 15 minutes. Release the clamp from each pan and remove the sides. Transfer the cakes and plates to a wire rack to cool completely.

Step 9

Using a large serrated knife, cut off the thin domed layer from the top of each cake. Creating a flat surface will help the cakes stack well.

TO MAKE THE BUTTERCREAM FROSTING

Step 10

In a large bowl, using a handheld electric mixer on medium speed, cream together the shortening and butter. Add the powdered sugar and vanilla. Mix, while slowly adding the heavy cream, until smooth and creamy.

Step 11

Frost the cake layers and outside of the cake as desired. Refrigerate leftovers, covered, for up to 5 days.

Chocolate Crack Pie

MAKES 1 (9-INCH) PIE
Prep time: 30 minutes, plus 30 minutes to chill
 Cook time: 40 minutes

Ingredients:

- Shortening, for preparing the pan

- 1 single Perfect Piecrust

- 125 grams All-Purpose Flour Blend

- 100 grams cane sugar or granulated sugar
- 100 grams light brown sugar
- ½ teaspoon xanthan gum
- 12 tablespoons (1½ sticks) butter or nondairy alternative
- 90 grams semisweet chocolate chips or nondairy alternative
- 2 large eggs
- 2 tablespoons whole milk or coconut milk beverage

Directions:

Step 1

Grease a 9-inch pie plate with shortening.

Step 2

Fit the piecrust into the prepared pie plate. Shape the edges. Refrigerate for at least 30 minutes.

Step 3

In a small bowl, whisk the flour, cane sugar, brown sugar, and xanthan gum to combine.

Step 4

Preheat the oven to 350°F.

Step 5

In a small saucepan, melt the butter over low heat. Add the chocolate chips. Cook, stirring, until melted. Remove the pan from the heat. Using a wooden spoon, immediately stir in the flour mixture until combined. Let stand 3 minutes to cool.

Step 6

Stir in the eggs and milk until smooth and creamy. Pour the filling into the chilled piecrust. If the oven is still preheating, place a piece of parchment paper on top of the pie and refrigerate it until the oven is ready.

Step 7

Bake for 35 to 40 minutes. or until the center does not jiggle.

Step 8

Let the pie cool completely before serving. Keep leftovers covered at room temperature, or refrigerate, for up to 5 days.

Perfect PiecrustSweet Blackberry Muffins

MAKES 12 MUFFINS
Prep time: 15 minutes
 Cook time: 25 minutes

Ingredients:

- 250 grams All-Purpose Flour Blend , plus 2 tablespoons, divided

- 2 teaspoons baking powder
- 1 teaspoon xanthan gum
- 1 teaspoon ground cinnamon
- ½ teaspoon ground nutmeg
- ½ teaspoon baking soda
- ½ teaspoon salt
- 100 grams cane sugar or granulated sugar, plus 4 teaspoons, divided
- 100 grams light brown sugar
- 6 tablespoons butter or nondairy alternative
- ½ cup whole milk or coconut milk beverage
- 80 grams vanilla Greek yogurt or nondairy alternative
- 2 large eggs
- 2 teaspoons vanilla extract
- ¼ teaspoon orange extract
- 230 grams blackberries

Directions:

Step 1

Preheat the oven to 425°F. Line a 12-cup muffin tin with cupcake liners.

Step 2

In a medium bowl, whisk 250 grams of flour, the baking powder, xanthan gum, cinnamon, nutmeg, baking soda, and salt to combine.

Step 3

In a small bowl, using a handheld electric mixer on medium speed, cream together 100 grams of cane sugar, the brown sugar, and butter until smooth. Beat in the milk, yogurt, eggs, vanilla, and orange extract until combined.

Step 4

In another small bowl, toss the blackberries with the remaining 2 tablespoons of flour and 1 teaspoon of cane sugar until well coated.

Step 5

Using a spatula, add the flour mixture to the butter mixture and mix until combined. Do not overmix. Gently fold in the blackberries. Evenly divide the batter between the prepared muffin cups. Smooth the tops of each muffin with your finger and sprinkle the remaining 3 teaspoons of sugar over the muffins.

Step 6

Bake for 5 minutes to let the muffins set, then (without opening the oven) reduce the oven temperature to 350°F and bake for 20 minutes more, or until a toothpick inserted into the center of a muffin comes out clean.

Step 7

Let the muffins cool in the pan for 10 minutes, then transfer them to a wire rack to cool completely. Keep the muffins covered for about 3 days at room temperature, or refrigerate, covered, for up to 5 days.

Oatmeal Blueberry Muffins

MAKES 12 MUFFINS
Prep time: 40 minutes
 Cook time: 25 minutes

Ingredients:

- 100 grams certified gluten-free rolled oats
- 1 cup whole milk or coconut milk beverage
- 1 teaspoon ground cinnamon
- 250 grams All-Purpose Flour Blend
- 2 teaspoons baking powder
- 1 teaspoon xanthan gum

- ½ teaspoon baking soda
- ½ teaspoon salt
- ½ cup avocado oil or canola oil
- ½ cup maple syrup
- 2 large eggs
- 2 teaspoons vanilla extract
- 100 grams blueberries

Directions:

Step 1

In a small bowl, stir together the oats, milk, and cinnamon. Let sit for 20 minutes, or until most of the milk has been absorbed. If needed, stir the oats and let soak for 10 minutes more.

Step 2

Preheat the oven to 425°F. Line a 12-cup muffin tin with cupcake liners.

Step 3

In a medium bowl, whisk the flour, baking powder, xanthan gum, baking soda, and salt to combine.

Step 4

In another medium bowl, whisk the oil, maple syrup, eggs, and vanilla until combined. Using a spatula, mix in the flour mixture. Add the soaked oats and mix again to combine. Gently fold in the blueberries. Evenly divide the batter between the prepared muffin cups.

Step 5

Bake for 5 minutes to let the muffins set, then (without opening the oven) reduce the oven temperature to 350°F and bake 20 minutes more, or until a toothpick inserted into the center of a muffin comes out clean.

Step 6

Let the muffins cool in the pan for 10 minutes, then transfer them to a wire rack to cool completely. Keep the muffins covered for about 3 days at room temperature or refrigerate for up to 5 days.

Apple Cinnamon Muffins

MAKES 12 MUFFINS

Prep time: 15 minutes
 Cook time: 25 minutes

Ingredients:

- 250 grams All-Purpose Flour Blend

- 3 teaspoons ground cinnamon, divided

- 2 teaspoons baking powder

- 1 teaspoon baking soda
- 1 teaspoon xanthan gum
- ½ teaspoon salt
- ½ teaspoon gluten-free apple pie spice
- 80 grams unsweetened applesauce
- ½ cup avocado oil or canola oil
- ½ cup maple syrup
- 2 large eggs
- 2 teaspoons vanilla extract
- 240 grams grated Granny Smith or Honeycrisp apple
- 1 tablespoon cane sugar or granulated sugar

Directions:

Step 1

Preheat the oven to 425°F. Line a 12-cup muffin tin with cupcake liners.

Step 2

In a medium bowl, whisk the flour, 2 teaspoons of cinnamon, the baking powder, baking soda, xanthan gum, salt, and apple pie spice to blend.

Step 3

In a large bowl, whisk the applesauce, oil, maple syrup, eggs, and vanilla until blended.

Step 4

Using a rubber spatula, blend half the flour mixture into the applesauce mixture to incorporate. Add the remaining flour mixture, folding until just combined. Do not overmix. Fold in the apple. Evenly divide the batter between the prepared muffin cups.

Step 5

In a small bowl, mix the sugar and remaining 1 teaspoon of cinnamon. Generously sprinkle the cinnamon sugar over each muffin.

Step 6

Bake for 5 minutes to let the muffins set, then (without opening the oven) reduce the oven temperature to 350°F and bake for 20 minutes more, or until a toothpick inserted into the center of a muffin comes out clean.

Step 7

Let the muffins cool in the pan for 10 minutes, then transfer them to a wire rack to cool completely. Store leftovers in an airtight container for about 3 days at room temperature, or refrigerate for up to 5 days.

Coffee Cake Muffins

MAKES 12 MUFFINS

Prep time: 15 minutes
Cook time: 25 minutes

Ingredients:

FOR THE TOPPING

- 4 tablespoons butter or nondairy alternative

- 125 grams All-Purpose Flour Blend

- ¼ teaspoon xanthan gum
- 50 grams cane sugar or granulated sugar
- 50 grams light brown sugar
- 1 teaspoon ground cinnamon
- ¼ teaspoon salt

FOR THE MUFFINS

- 250 grams All-Purpose Flour Blend

- 2 teaspoons baking powder
- 1 teaspoon xanthan gum
- 1 teaspoon ground cinnamon
- ½ teaspoon baking soda
- ¼ teaspoon salt
- 100 grams light brown sugar
- ¾ cup whole milk or coconut milk beverage
- ⅓ cup avocado oil or canola oil
- 2 large eggs
- 2 teaspoons vanilla extract

FOR THE GLAZE

- 30 grams powdered sugar
- 1 teaspoon whole milk or coconut milk beverage
- ½ teaspoon vanilla extract

Directions:

Step 1

Preheat the oven to 425°F. Line a 12-cup muffin tin with cupcake liners.

TO MAKE THE TOPPING

Step 2

In a small saucepan, melt the butter over low heat. Set aside to cool.

Step 3

In a small bowl, whisk the flour and xanthan gum to blend. Add the cane sugar, brown sugar, cinnamon, and salt. Slowly pour in the melted butter, whisking. Do not use a spatula (which would make the mixture creamy); the whisk will separate the ingredients to produce a crumb consistency. Spread the topping on a piece of parchment paper to dry.

TO MAKE THE MUFFINS

Step 4

In a medium bowl, whisk the flour, baking powder, xanthan gum, cinnamon, baking soda, salt, and brown sugar to combine.

Step 5

In a large bowl, using a whisk or handheld electric mixer on medium speed, combine the milk, oil, eggs, and vanilla.

Step 6

Add half of the flour mixture to the milk mixture, mix them on low speed, then add the remaining half of the flour mixture and mix just until a batter is formed. Do not overmix. Evenly divide the batter between the prepared muffin cups.

Step 7

Generously sprinkle each muffin with the topping and gently pat it down with your fingertips.

Step 8

Bake for 5 minutes to let the muffins set, then (without opening the oven) reduce the oven temperature to 350°F and bake for 20 minutes more, or until a toothpick inserted into the center of a muffin comes out clean.

Step 9

Let the muffins cool in the pan for 10 minutes, then transfer them to a wire rack to cool completely.

TO MAKE THE GLAZE

Step 10

While the muffins cool, in a small bowl, whisk the powdered sugar, milk, and vanilla until smooth.

Step 11

Drizzle the glaze over each cooled muffin. Store leftover muffins in an airtight container for about 3 days at room temperature, or refrigerate for up to 5 days.

Veggie Muffins

MAKES 12 MUFFINS
Prep time: 30 minutes
Cook time: 25 minutes

Ingredients:

- 150 grams grated zucchini (about 2 small zucchini)

- 250 grams All-Purpose Flour Blend

- 2 teaspoons ground cinnamon
- 2 teaspoons baking powder
- 1 teaspoon xanthan gum
- ½ teaspoon baking soda
- ½ teaspoon salt
- ¼ teaspoon ground nutmeg
- 100 grams cane sugar or granulated sugar
- ½ cup avocado oil or canola oil
- 2 large eggs
- 2 teaspoons vanilla extract
- 55 grams grated carrot (about 2 carrots)

Directions:

Step 1

Preheat the oven to 425°F. Line a 12-cup muffin tin with cupcake liners.

Step 2

Place the grated zucchini between 2 paper towels to absorb most of the moisture.

Step 3

In a medium bowl, whisk the flour, cinnamon, baking powder, xanthan gum, baking soda, salt, and nutmeg to combine.

Step 4

In a small bowl, whisk the sugar, oil, eggs, and vanilla to blend. Using a spatula, add the flour mixture and mix until combined. Do not overmix. Using a spatula, fold in the zucchini and carrots. Evenly divide the batter between the prepared muffin cups.

Step 5

Bake for 5 minutes to let the muffins set, then (without opening the oven) reduce the oven temperature to 350°F and bake for 20 minutes, or until a toothpick inserted into the center of a muffin comes out clean.

Step 6

Let the muffins cool in the pan for 10 minutes, then transfer them to a wire rack to cool completely. Serve warm or cool. Keep covered at room temperature for up to 3 days or refrigerate for up to 5 days. You can also freeze them in a freezer bag. Let them thaw naturally or place in a 350°F oven for 5 to 7 minutes to warm.

Easy Drop Biscuits

MAKES 12 BISCUITS

Prep time: 15 minutes
 Cook time: 15 minutes

Ingredients:

- Shortening, for preparing the pan

- 375 grams All-Purpose Flour Blend

- 2 tablespoons baking powder
- 2 teaspoons cane sugar or granulated sugar
- 1½ teaspoons xanthan gum
- ½ teaspoon salt
- 6 tablespoons cold butter, divided
- 102 grams shortening
- 1 large egg
- 1 tablespoon honey, plus 2 teaspoons
- 1½ cups buttermilk, or 1½ cups coconut milk beverage plus 1½ tablespoons apple cider vinegar (see here)

Directions:

Step 1

Preheat the oven to 425°F. Grease a 12-cup muffin-top pan (yes, a pan that just makes muffin tops) with a light coating of shortening. (Or line a baking sheet with parchment paper.)

Step 2

In the bowl of a food processor, combine the flour, baking powder, sugar, xanthan gum, and salt and pulse about 5 times. Cut 4 tablespoons of butter into small pieces and add it to the food processor. Add the shortening in 3 portions, pulsing after each addition until a sand-like consistency forms.

Step 3

Add the egg, 2 teaspoons of honey, and ¾ cup of buttermilk. As you pulse the machine, drizzle the remaining ¾ cup of buttermilk through the feed tube. Keep pulsing until a thick batter forms. You may want to give it a stir to make sure the bottom ingredients are completely mixed in.

Step 4

Using a 2-tablespoon ice cream scoop, portion the batter into the prepared muffin-top cups. (Or place them about 2 inches apart on the lined baking sheet.)

Step 5

Bake for 13 to 15 minutes, or until the edges begin to brown.

Step 6

While the biscuits bake, in a small saucepan, melt the remaining 2 tablespoons of butter and 1 tablespoon of honey over medium-low heat.

Step 7

As soon as the biscuits come out of the oven, using a pastry brush, brush them with the honey-butter topping. Serve warm. These biscuits are best served same day, but you can refrigerate leftovers in an airtight container for up to 3 days, or freeze for up to 1 month. Warm in a 350°F oven for 5 to 7 minutes.

Garlic and Herb Drop Biscuits

MAKES 12 BISCUITS

Prep time: 15 minutes

 Cook time: 25 minutes

Ingredients:

- Shortening for preparing the pan

- 6 tablespoons cold butter or nondairy alternative, divided
- 2½ teaspoons garlic powder, divided

- 375 grams All-Purpose Flour Blend

- 2 tablespoons baking powder
- 1½ teaspoons xanthan gum
- 1 teaspoon salt
- 1½ teaspoons dried oregano
- ½ teaspoon dried parsley
- ½ teaspoon dried thyme
- 6 to 8 fresh basil leaves, chopped
- 102 grams shortening
- 1 large egg
- 2 teaspoons honey
- 1½ cups buttermilk, or 1½ cups coconut milk beverage plus 1½ tablespoons apple cider vinegar (see here)

Directions:

Step 1

Preheat the oven to 425°F. Grease a 12-cup muffin-top pan (yes, a pan that just makes muffin tops) with shortening. (Or line a baking sheet with parchment paper.)

Step 2

In a small saucepan, melt 2 tablespoons of butter over low heat. Add 1 teaspoon of garlic powder. Bring the mixture to a boil and cook until the garlic is completely dissolved, about 3 minutes. Remove from the heat and set the garlic butter aside.

Step 3

In the bowl of a food processor, combine the flour, baking powder, xanthan gum, salt, remaining 1½ teaspoons of garlic powder, oregano, parsley, thyme, and basil and pulse about 5 times. Cut the remaining 4 tablespoons of butter into small pieces and add it to the food processor. Add the shortening in 3 portions, pulsing after each addition until a sand-like consistency forms.

Step 4

Add the egg, honey, and ¾ cup of buttermilk. As you pulse the machine, drizzle the remaining ¾ cup of buttermilk through the feed tube, pulsing until a thick batter forms. Give it a stir to make sure the bottom ingredients are completely mixed in.

Step 5

Using a 2-tablespoon ice cream scoop, portion the batter into the prepared muffin cups. (Or place them a few inches apart on the lined baking sheet.)

Step 6

Bake for 13 minutes. Remove from the oven and, using a pastry brush, immediately brush with some of the garlic butter. Bake for 3 to 5 minutes more, or until the edges begin to brown.

Step 7

Immediately remove and brush the biscuits again with the remaining garlic butter. Serve warm. Refrigerate leftovers in an airtight container for up to 3 days, or freeze for up to 1 month. Warm in a 350°F oven for 5 to 7 minutes.

Classic Biscuits

MAKES 6 BISCUITS

Prep time: 45 minutes
 Cook time: 15 minutes

Ingredients:

- 136 grams shortening
- 312 grams All-Purpose Flour Blend , plus more for dusting
- 2 tablespoons baking powder
- 1 teaspoon xanthan gum
- 1 teaspoon baking soda
- 1 teaspoon salt
- 2 teaspoons cane sugar or granulated sugar
- 1 large egg
- 1 cup buttermilk, or 1 cup coconut milk beverage plus 1 tablespoon apple cider vinegar (see here), chilled, divided
- 2 tablespoons butter or nondairy alternative
- 1 tablespoon honey

Directions:

Step 1

Place the shortening in a small bowl and freeze for at least 30 minutes.

Step 2

Preheat the oven to 475°F. For best results, use a well-seasoned cast-iron skillet. (Or line a baking sheet with parchment paper.)

Step 3

In a medium bowl, whisk the flour, baking powder, xanthan gum, baking soda, salt, and sugar to combine. Add the cold shortening and use a pastry cutter to cut it into the flour mixture until you have a very coarse crumb.

Step 4

Place two sheets of parchment paper on a work surface and dust them well with flour.

Step 5

Make a well in the center of the flour mixture and add the egg and ¾ cup of chilled buttermilk. Using a spatula, fold the dough together. The less you touch the dough by hand, the better. The dough will seem crumbly; that's okay. Transfer the dough to the floured work surface. Pat the dough into a rectangle about 1 inch thick.

Step 6

Fold the dough into thirds, bringing in the left and right sides. This is called laminating the dough to produce layers. Next, fold in the top and bottom sides. Repeat this process one more time. Shape the dough into one last rectangle, about 6 by 9 inches and 1 inch thick.

Step 7

Place the second piece of parchment on top of the biscuit dough and gently smooth the top using a rolling pin, without flattening the rectangle. Using a 3-inch square cutter, cut out 6 biscuits. The biscuits are square so they touch and stick to each other to help them expand and rise. Rounds will not give you the same results. Transfer the biscuits to the skillet, placing them so they touch.

Step 8

Using a pastry brush, brush the tops with a light coating of the remaining buttermilk (you might not use all of it).

Step 9

Bake for 15 minutes, or until the biscuits turn lightly golden.

Step 10

While the biscuits bake, in a small saucepan, combine the butter and honey and melt over medium-low heat.

Step 11

Brush the honey butter over the biscuits as soon as they come out of the oven. They are best served warm the same day, with jam, butter, or bacon. They can also be frozen in a freezer bag for up to 1 month.

Lemon-Glazed Blackberry Scones

MAKES 8 SCONES

Prep time: 1 hour

 Cook time: 25 minutes

Ingredients:

FOR THE SCONES

- 115 grams blackberries, halved
- 3 tablespoons butter, frozen, plus 2 tablespoons, melted and slightly chilled
- 68 grams shortening
- 250 grams All-Purpose Flour Blend , plus 32 grams for dusting
- ½ cup buttermilk, or ½ cup coconut milk beverage plus 1½ teaspoons apple cider vinegar (see here)
- 60 grams vanilla Greek yogurt or nondairy alternative
- 1 large egg
- 100 grams cane sugar or granulated sugar
- 2 teaspoons baking powder
- 1 teaspoon baking soda
- 1 teaspoon xanthan gum
- ½ teaspoon salt
- 2 tablespoons grated lemon zest (about 2 large lemons)

FOR THE LEMON GLAZE

- 210 grams powdered sugar
- 2 tablespoons grated lemon zest (about 2 large lemons)
- 2½ tablespoons fresh lemon juice

Directions:

TO MAKE THE SCONES

Step 1

Place the blackberries in a bowl and into the freezer to chill.

Step 2

Grate the frozen butter into a small bowl and add the shortening. Place back into the freezer for at least 30 minutes.

Step 3

Place a large piece of parchment paper on a work surface and dust it with flour (you won't use all 32 grams at once—start with a little and add more as needed).

Step 4

In a small bowl, whisk the buttermilk, yogurt, and egg to blend. Refrigerate until needed

Step 5

In a medium bowl, whisk the remaining 250 grams of flour, the sugar, baking powder, baking soda, xanthan gum, salt, and lemon zest to combine. Add the cold butter and shortening and use a pastry cutter to cut it into the flour mixture until you have a coarse crumb. Don't overdo it. It's okay to have some bigger chunks.

Step 6

Add the buttermilk mixture and form the dough with your clean hands. Transfer the dough to the floured work surface and flatten it into a square, then fold in the edges. Flatten again and fold in the edges one more time. The folding creates the flaky layers. Use extra flour and a bench scraper (if you have one) to help you lift each side if the dough gets sticky.

Step 7

Create a large rectangle about 5 by 14 inches, and place the blackberries in the center. Gently press them into the dough. Fold in all sides one last time and create a 3-by-12-inch rectangle.

Step 8

Trim the parchment paper if necessary, leaving plenty of space around the rectangle, and brush off any remaining flour. Using the parchment, transfer the rectangle onto a baking sheet and refrigerate for 30 minutes.

Step 9

Preheat the oven to 425°F. Line a new baking sheet with parchment paper.

Step 10

Using a sharp knife or bench scraper, cut the rectangle into 4 equal squares. Then cut each square diagonally to form triangles. Avoid using a sawing motion. Push your knife down, then lift up. Using the bench scraper, gently transfer each scone to the prepared baking sheet, leaving space between them. Using a pastry brush, brush each scone with melted butter.

Step 11

Bake for 15 to 25 minutes, or until the corners look crisp.

Step 12

Let the scones cool on the pan for 10 minutes, then transfer them to a wire rack until just warm, or cooled completely.

TO MAKE THE LEMON GLAZE

Step 13

In a small bowl, stir together the powdered sugar, lemon zest, and lemon juice until smooth.

Step 14

Drizzle the glaze over the scones and serve. Keep the scones covered at room temperature for 2 days, or refrigerated for up to 4 days.

Orange Cranberry Scones

MAKES 8 SCONES

Prep time: 1 hour
 Cook time: 25 minutes

Ingredients:

- 3 tablespoons butter, frozen, plus 2 tablespoons, melted and slightly cooled
- 68 grams shortening
- ½ cup buttermilk, or ½ cup coconut milk beverage plus 1½ teaspoons apple cider vinegar (see here)
- 40 grams vanilla Greek yogurt or nondairy alternative
- 1 large egg
- ½ teaspoon orange extract
- 250 grams All-Purpose Flour Blend , plus 32 grams for dusting
- 100 grams cane sugar or granulated sugar, plus more for sprinkling
- 2 teaspoons baking powder
- 1 teaspoon baking soda
- 1 teaspoon xanthan gum
- ½ teaspoon salt
- 2 tablespoons grated orange zest (about 1 large orange)
- 100 grams frozen cranberries (do not thaw)

Directions:

Step 1

Grate the frozen butter into a small bowl and add the shortening. Place back into the freezer for at least 30 minutes.

Step 2

In a small bowl, whisk the buttermilk, yogurt, egg, and orange extract to blend. Refrigerate until needed.

Step 3

In a medium bowl, whisk the flour, sugar, baking powder, baking soda, xanthan gum, salt, and orange zest to combine. Add the cold butter and shortening and use a pastry cutter to cut it into the flour mixture until you have a coarse crumb. Don't overdo it. It's okay to have some bigger chunks.

Step 4

Place a large piece of parchment paper on a work surface and dust it with flour (you won't use all 32 grams at once—start with a little and add more as needed).

Step 5

Add the egg mixture to the flour mixture and form the dough with your clean hands. Transfer the dough to the floured work surface. Flatten the dough into a square and fold in all sides. Fold in the sides again and repeat. Use the extra flour and a bench scraper (if you have one) to help you lift each side if the dough gets sticky. The folding creates the flaky layers.

Step 6

Create a rectangle about 5 by 14 inches and place the cranberries in the center. Gently press them into the dough. Fold in all sides and create a 3-by-12-inch rectangle. Trim the parchment paper if necessary, leaving plenty of space around the rectangle, and brush off any remaining flour. Using the parchment, transfer the rectangle onto a baking sheet and refrigerate for 30 minutes.

Step 7

Preheat the oven to 425°F. Line a new baking sheet with parchment paper.

Step 8

Using a sharp knife or bench scraper, cut the rectangle into 4 equal squares. Then cut each square diagonally to form triangles. Avoid using a sawing motion. Push your knife down, then lift up. Using the bench scraper, gently transfer each scone to the prepared baking sheet, leaving space between them.

Step 9

Using a pastry brush, brush each scone with the melted butter. Sprinkle the tops with a little sugar.

Step 10

Bake for 15 to 25 minutes, or until the corners look crisp.

Step 11

Let the scones cool on the pan for 10 minutes, then transfer them to a wire rack to cool completely. Keep covered at room temperature for 2 days, or refrigerate for up to 4 days.

Cheddar Bacon Breakfast Scones

MAKES 8 SCONES

Prep time: 1 hour

 Cook time: 25 minutes

Ingredients:

- 3 tablespoons butter, frozen, plus 1 tablespoon, melted and slightly cooled

- 68 grams shortening
- 250 grams All-Purpose Flour Blend , plus 32 grams for dusting
- ½ cup buttermilk, or ½ cup coconut milk beverage plus 1½ teaspoons apple cider vinegar (see here)
- 60 grams vanilla Greek yogurt or nondairy alternative
- 1 large egg
- 50 grams cane sugar or granulated sugar
- 2 teaspoons baking powder

- 1 teaspoon baking soda
- 1 teaspoon xanthan gum
- ½ teaspoon salt
- 60 grams shredded cheddar cheese, plus 2 tablespoons, or nondairy alternative
- 225 grams cooked crumbled bacon

Directions:

Step 1

Grate the frozen butter into a small bowl and add the shortening. Place back into the freezer for at least 30 minutes.

Step 2

Place a large piece of parchment paper on a work surface and dust it with flour (you won't use all 32 grams at once—start with a little and add more as needed).

Step 3

In another small bowl, whisk the buttermilk, yogurt, and egg to blend. Refrigerate until needed

Step 4

In a medium bowl, whisk the remaining 250 grams of flour, the sugar, baking powder, baking soda, xanthan gum, salt, and 60 grams of cheddar. Add the cold butter and shortening and use a pastry cutter to cut it into the flour mixture until you have coarse crumbs. Don't overdo it. It's okay to have some bigger chunks.

Step 5

Add the egg mixture and form the dough with your clean hands. Transfer the dough to the floured work surface and flatten it into a square, folding in the sides. Flatten the dough and fold in the sides again. The folding creates the flaky layers. Use the extra flour and a bench scraper (if you have one) to help you lift each side if the dough gets sticky.

Step 6

Create a large rectangle about 5 by 14 inches. Reserve 2 tablespoons of the bacon and place the remaining bacon in the center of the rectangle. Gently press the bacon into the dough and fold in the sides one last time to make a 3-by-12-inch rectangle.

Step 7

Trim the parchment paper, if needed, leaving plenty of space around the rectangle, and brush off any remaining flour. Using the parchment, transfer the rectangle onto a baking sheet and refrigerate for 30 minutes.

Step 8

Preheat the oven to 425°F. Line a new baking sheet with parchment paper.

Step 9

Mince the reserved bacon and remaining 2 tablespoons of cheddar.

Step 10

Using a sharp knife or bench scraper, cut the rectangle into 4 equal squares. Then cut each square diagonally to form triangles. Avoid using a sawing motion. Push your knife down, then lift up. Using the bench scraper, gently transfer each scone to the prepared baking sheet, leaving space between them.

Step 11

Using a pastry brush, brush each scone with melted butter. Sprinkle the minced bacon and cheddar on top.

Step 12

Bake for 15 to 25 minutes, or until the corners look crisp.

Step 13

Let the scones cool on the pan for 10 minutes. These scones are best served warm. Keep covered at room temperature for 2 days, or refrigerate for up to 4 days.

Pepperoni Pizza Scones

MAKES 8 SCONES

Prep time: 40 minutes

Cook time: 25 minutes

Ingredients:

- 3 tablespoons butter, frozen, plus 2 tablespoons

- 68 grams shortening
- 56 grams plus 2 tablespoons gluten-free pepperoni, diced
- 50 grams plus 2 tablespoons shredded mozzarella cheese or nondairy alternative
- 2 teaspoons dried oregano
- 4 or 5 fresh basil leaves, chopped
- 25 grams dry-packed sun-dried tomatoes, diced
- 1 teaspoon garlic powder
- 250 grams All-Purpose Flour Blend , plus 32 grams for dusting
- ½ cup buttermilk, or ½ cup coconut milk beverage plus 1½ teaspoons apple cider vinegar (see here)
- 40 grams vanilla Greek yogurt or nondairy alternative
- 1 large egg
- 50 grams cane sugar or granulated sugar
- 2 teaspoons baking powder
- 1 teaspoon baking soda
- 1 teaspoon xanthan gum
- ½ teaspoon salt

Directions:

Step 1

Grate the frozen butter into a small bowl and add the shortening. Place back into the freezer for at least 30 minutes.

Step 2

In a small bowl, stir together the pepperoni, mozzarella, oregano, and basil. Measure out 2 tablespoons and set aside.

Step 3

Add the sun-dried tomatoes to the pepperoni mixture and stir to combine.

Step 4

In a small skillet, melt the remaining 2 tablespoons of butter over medium-low heat. Add the garlic powder and simmer until it completely dissolves.

Step 5

Place a large piece of parchment paper on a work surface and dust it with flour (you won't use all 32 grams at once—start with a little and add more as needed).

Step 6

In another small bowl, whisk the buttermilk, yogurt, and egg to blend. Refrigerate until needed.

Step 7

In a medium bowl, stir together the remaining 250 grams of flour, the sugar, baking powder, baking soda, xanthan gum, salt, and pepperoni/sun-dried tomato mixture. Add the frozen butter and shortening and use a pastry cutter to cut it into the flour mixture until coarse crumbs form. Don't overdo it. It's okay to have some bigger chunks.

Step 8

Add the egg mixture and form the dough with your clean hands. Transfer the dough to the floured work surface. Flatten it into a square and fold in the sides. Flatten the dough and fold in the sides again. The folding creates the flaky layers. Use the extra flour and a bench scraper (if you have one) to lift each side if the dough gets sticky. Fold in the sides one last time to make a 3-by-12-inch rectangle.

Step 9

Trim the parchment, if needed, leaving plenty of space around the rectangle, and brush off any remaining flour. Using the parchment, transfer the rectangle onto a baking sheet and refrigerate for 30 minutes.

Step 10

Preheat the oven to 425°F. Line a new baking sheet with parchment paper.

Step 11

Use a sharp knife to cut the rectangle into 4 equal squares. Cut each square diagonally to form triangles. Using the bench scraper, gently transfer each scone to the prepared baking sheet, leaving space between them.

Step 12

Using a pastry brush, brush each scone with the melted garlic butter. Sprinkle the reserved 2 tablespoons of pepperoni mixture on top.

Step 13

Bake for 15 to 25 minutes, or until the corners look crisp.

Step 14

Let the scones cool on the pan for 10 minutes. Serve warm. Keep covered at room temperature for 2 days, or refrigerate for up to 4 days.

MAKES 1 (9-INCH) GALETTE

Prep time: 1 hour 30 minutes
 Cook time: about 1 hour

Ingredients:

- All-Purpose Flour Blend , for dusting

- 1 double Perfect Piecrust

- 1½ pounds heirloom tomatoes, thinly sliced
- 2 garlic cloves, minced
- 1 teaspoon salt
- ½ teaspoon freshly ground black pepper
- 60 grams Gouda or cheddar cheese or nondairy alternative, grated
- 1 tablespoon grated Parmesan cheese or nondairy alternative
- 4 fresh basil leaves, halved
- 1 large egg
- 1 teaspoon dried oregano
- ½ teaspoon red pepper flakes

Directions:

Step 1

Line a baking sheet with parchment paper. Dust a work surface with flour. Weigh out 500 grams of the pie dough, about two-thirds of the full recipe (save the rest for kids' treats; see Tip). Roll the dough into a round about 12 inches across and a little more than ⅛ inch thick. Transfer the dough to the prepared baking sheet and refrigerate for at least 1 hour.

Step 2

Preheat the oven to 400°F. Line a baking sheet with aluminum foil. Line a large plate with paper towels.

Step 3

Arrange the tomato slices in a single layer on the prepared baking sheet and sprinkle with the garlic, salt, and pepper.

Step 4

Bake for 5 minutes. The tomatoes will start releasing some juice. Drain off the juice and transfer the tomatoes to the paper towels.

Step 5

Remove the dough from the refrigerator and let sit for a minute to soften. Sprinkle the Gouda and Parmesan over the dough, leaving a clean 1½-inch border all around. Place the tomatoes over the cheese. Arrange the basil evenly on top. Bring the edges of the dough up and over the filling, overlapping pieces, as needed, to create a border that is 1½ inches wide.

Step 6

In a small bowl, whisk the egg and 1 tablespoon water to create an egg wash. Using a pastry brush, brush the egg wash over the border.

Step 7

Freeze the galette for 10 minutes.

Step 8

Bake for 55 to 60 minutes, or until the crust is golden brown.

Step 9

Let the galette cool slightly. Sprinkle with the oregano and red pepper flakes. Serve warm. Refrigerate leftovers in an airtight container for up to 3 days.

Crunchy Caramel Apple Pie

MAKES 1 (9-INCH) PIE
Prep time: 45 minutes
Cook time: 55 minutes

Ingredients:

FOR THE PIECRUST

- Shortening, for preparing the pan
- 1 single Perfect Piecrust

FOR THE FILLING

- 100 grams cane sugar or granulated sugar
- 32 grams All-Purpose Flour Blend
- 1 teaspoon ground cinnamon

- ¼ teaspoon xanthan gum
- ¼ teaspoon salt
- 720 grams very thinly sliced peeled Honeycrisp or Granny Smith apples

FOR THE CRUMBLE TOPPING AND DRIZZLE

- 200 grams light brown sugar

- 62 grams All-Purpose Flour Blend

- 50 grams certified gluten-free rolled oats
- ¼ teaspoon xanthan gum
- 8 tablespoons (1 stick) cold butter or nondairy alternative
- 31 grams chopped pecans
- ¼ cup salted caramel sauce (from Salted Caramel Brownies)

Directions:

TO MAKE THE PIECRUST

Step 1

Preheat the oven to 375°F. Lightly grease a 9-inch pie plate with shortening.

Step 2

Roll out and fit the piecrust into the prepared plate as directed and refrigerate it.

TO MAKE THE FILLING

Step 3

In a large bowl, whisk the cane sugar, flour, cinnamon, xanthan gum, and salt to combine. Using a spatula, fold in the apples, covering them completely in the flour mixture.

Step 4

Remove the piecrust from the refrigerator and pour the apple mixture into it. Return it to the refrigerator.

TO MAKE THE CRUMBLE TOPPING

Step 5

In a medium bowl, whisk the brown sugar, flour, oats, and xanthan gum to combine. Cut the butter into pieces and add it to the oat mixture. Using a pastry cutter, cut the butter into the oats until coarse crumbs form.

Step 6

Remove the filled crust from the refrigerator and cover it evenly with the crumble topping. Loosely cover the edges of the crust with aluminum foil.

Step 7

Bake for 25 minutes. Remove the foil and bake for 25 to 30 minutes more, or until the filling is bubbling and the crust is golden.

Step 8

Transfer to a wire rack to cool.

TO FINISH THE PIE

Step 9

Sprinkle the pie with pecans and drizzle the salted caramel sauce over the top. Refrigerate leftovers, covered, for up to 3 days.

MAKES 1 (9-INCH) DOUBLE PIECRUST OR 2 (9-INCH) SINGLE PIECRUSTS

Prep time: 1 hour

Ingredients:

- 136 grams chilled shortening
- 8 tablespoons (1 stick) butter or nondairy alternative
- 250 grams All-Purpose Flour Blend , plus more for dusting
- 63 grams brown rice flour
- 63 grams sorghum flour
- 1½ teaspoons xanthan gum
- 1 teaspoon salt
- 1 large egg
- 1 tablespoon apple cider vinegar
- 2 to 3 tablespoons ice-cold water

Directions:

Step 1

Freeze the shortening and butter for at least 30 minutes.

Step 2

Place two sheets of parchment paper on a work surface and dust them with the all-purpose flour.

Step 3

In a medium bowl, whisk the all-purpose flour, rice flour, sorghum flour, xanthan gum, and salt to combine.

Step 4

Cut the cold butter into pieces and add it and the cold shortening to the flour mixture. Using a pastry cutter, cut the fats into the flour until a crumbly mixture forms. Add the egg, vinegar, and 2 tablespoons of ice-cold water. Mix the dough, adding the remaining 1 tablespoon of ice-cold water, as needed, until a smooth dough forms.

Step 5

Divide the dough into 2 portions. Place one portion on a floured sheet of parchment and put the second sheet of parchment on top. Roll the dough into a 12-inch round a little less than ¼ inch thick.

Step 6

Remove the top sheet of parchment and flip the dough into the pie plate. Push down from the edges (not the middle) to create slack. Gently fit the dough into the bottom and sides of the plate. Remove the remaining piece of parchment. Smooth and crimp the edges of the crust, as desired. Refrigerate for at least 30 minutes before baking.

Step 7

Repeat steps 5 and 6 with the second dough portion either to make a second bottom crust or to roll it into an 11-inch round for a top crust.

Blueberry Crumble Slab Pie

MAKES 1 (9-BY-13-INCH) SLAB PIE

Prep time: 50 minutes

Cook time: 30 minutes

Ingredients:

FOR THE CRUST

- Shortening, for preparing the pan
- 313 grams All-Purpose Flour Blend , plus more for dusting
- 1 teaspoon xanthan gum
- 1 teaspoon salt
- 12 tablespoons (1½ sticks) cold butter or nondairy alternative
- 8 to 10 tablespoons ice-cold water

FOR THE FILLING

- 200 grams cane sugar or granulated sugar
- 32 grams All-Purpose Flour Blend
- ¼ teaspoon xanthan gum
- 600 grams blueberries
- 1 tablespoon fresh lemon juice

FOR THE CRUMBLE TOPPING

- 100 grams certified gluten-free rolled oats
- 200 grams light brown sugar
- 62 grams All-Purpose Flour Blend

- 1 teaspoon ground cinnamon
- ¼ teaspoon xanthan gum
- 8 tablespoons (1 stick) butter or nondairy alternative
- 62 grams chopped pecans (optional)

Directions:

TO MAKE THE CRUST

Step 1

Line a 9-by-13-inch jelly-roll pan with aluminum foil and lightly grease it with shortening. Place two sheets of parchment paper on a work surface and dust them with flour.

Step 2

In a medium bowl, whisk the flour, xanthan gum, and salt to combine.

Step 3

Cut the butter into small pieces and add it to the flour mixture. Using a pastry cutter, cut the butter into the flour mixture until crumbs form.

Step 4

Add 2 tablespoons of ice-cold water as you form the dough by hand. Continue to add the water, 1 tablespoon at a time, until the dough is smooth. Transfer the dough to the floured work surface and divide it into 2 portions.

Step 5

Roll 1 portion of the dough between the two parchment sheets to about ⅛ inch thick. Remove the top sheet of parchment. Flip the dough into one side of the prepared pan using the technique from my Perfect Piecrust (step 6).

Step 6

Repeat rolling the second dough portion and flip it into the other side of the pan so both pieces overlap in the center. Use your fingers to connect them and smooth the surface. Trim and crimp the edges. Refrigerate the crust for at least 30 minutes while you prepare the filling and topping.

TO MAKE THE FILLING

Step 7

In a small bowl, whisk the sugar, flour, and xanthan gum to combine.

Step 8

Place the blueberries in a large bowl and sprinkle them with lemon juice. Stir to be sure all the berries are coated in the juice. Add the flour mixture and stir again to coat.

TO MAKE THE CRUMBLE TOPPING

Step 9

Preheat the oven to 375°F.

Step 10

In a medium bowl, whisk the oats, brown sugar, flour, cinnamon, and xanthan gum to combine. Using a pastry cutter, cut the butter into the flour mixture until crumbs form. Stir in the pecans (if using).

Step 11

Remove the chilled crust from the refrigerator and pour the filling over it. Sprinkle the crumble on top.

Step 12

Bake for 30 minutes, or until the blueberries are bubbling.

Step 13

Serve warm or cold. Keep leftovers covered at room temperature for 2 days, or refrigerate for up to 4 days.

Coconut Cream Pie

MAKES 1 (9-INCH) PIE

Prep time: 1 hour 25 minutes, plus 3 hours to chill
 Cook time: 27 minutes

Ingredients:

- 200 grams shredded coconut, divided

- Shortening, for preparing the pie plate

- 1 single Perfect Piecrust

- 4 large egg yolks
- 1 teaspoon vanilla extract

- 125 grams All-Purpose Flour Blend

- ¼ teaspoon xanthan gum
- ¼ teaspoon salt
- 1 (14-ounce) can coconut cream
- 1 cup cold whole milk or coconut milk beverage
- 133 grams cane sugar or granulated sugar
- 2 tablespoons butter or nondairy alternative
- Whipped cream or nondairy alternative, for serving

Directions:

Step 1

Preheat the oven to 325°F. Line a baking sheet with parchment paper.

Step 2

Spread 100 grams of coconut into a thin layer on the prepared baking sheet. Bake for 5 to 7 minutes, or until golden. Set the coconut aside until serving time.

Step 3

Coat a 9-inch pie plate with shortening and fit the piecrust into the pie plate. Shape the edges to your liking. Refrigerate for 1 hour.

Step 4

Preheat the oven to 400°F.

Step 5

Line the piecrust with parchment or aluminum foil (shiny-side down) and fill the bottom with dried beans or pie weights. Blind bake the crust for about 15 minutes, or until the edges are golden. Remove from the oven and remove the lining and weights. Prick holes all over the bottom of the crust with a fork. Return to the oven for 10 to 12 minutes, until the crust begins to brown. Let it cool completely as you prepare the filling.

Step 6

In a medium bowl, whisk the egg yolks and vanilla. In a small bowl, whisk together the flour, xanthan gum, and salt.

Step 7

In a large saucepan, whisk the coconut cream, milk, and sugar together over medium heat. Bring it to a boil, whisking occasionally, for about 2 minutes, then remove from the heat.

Step 8

Whisk the flour mixture into the egg mixture. Then, whisking constantly, use a ladle to slowly add a small and steady stream of the warm cream mixture to the flour/egg mixture. Keep whisking so the egg yolks do not scramble. Repeat with one more ladle of cream mixture.

Step 9

Return the saucepan to low heat and combine all of the mixture into it. Bring to a simmer for 3 to 4 minutes, or until the mixture is bubbling and thickened slightly.

Step 10

Remove the saucepan from the heat and stir in the butter and remaining 100 grams of coconut.

Step 11

Pour the filling into the baked piecrust and cover it tightly with plastic (the plastic should be touching the filling). Chill the pie for at least 3 hours or overnight for best results.

Step 12

Serve the pie topped with whipped cream and sprinkled with the toasted coconut. This pie is best served cold. Refrigerate leftovers, covered, for up to 3 days.

The Great Pumpkin Pie

MAKES 1 (9-INCH) PIE

Prep time: 30 minutes

 Cook time: about 1 hour 10 minutes

Ingredients:

FOR THE PIECRUST

* Shortening, for preparing the pie plate

* 1 double Perfect Piecrust

FOR THE FILLING

* 20 grams All-Purpose Flour Blend

* 2 teaspoons ground cinnamon
* ½ teaspoon salt
* ¼ teaspoon ground nutmeg
* ¼ teaspoon ground cloves
* ¼ teaspoon xanthan gum
* Sprinkle freshly ground black pepper
* 4 large eggs, divided
* 1 (**Step 7**4-ounce) can sweetened condensed coconut milk
* ¼ cup maple syrup
* 1 (15-ounce) can pumpkin puree

FOR THE COCONUT WHIPPED CREAM

* 1 (14-ounce) can coconut cream, refrigerated overnight
* 2 tablespoons powdered sugar

Directions:

TO MAKE THE PIECRUST

Step 1

Preheat the oven to 425°F. Lightly grease a 9-inch pie plate with shortening. Line a baking sheet with parchment paper.

Step 2

Prepare the dough and roll out one portion as directed. Fit the dough round into the pie plate as directed and crimp the edges.

Step 3

Roll out the second portion and place it on the prepared baking sheet. Refrigerate both crusts while you make the filling.

TO MAKE THE FILLING

Step 4

In a small bowl, whisk the flour, cinnamon, salt, nutmeg, cloves, xanthan gum, and pepper to combine.

Step 5

In a large bowl, whisk 3 of the eggs and the condensed milk until smooth and creamy with zero lumps. Using a spatula, stir in the maple syrup until combined. (I do not recommend using a handheld electric mixer for this step.) Add the flour mixture and pumpkin and stir again just until combined with no lumps, stopping to scrape the edges of the bowl, as needed. Do not overmix.

Step 6

Remove the bottom crust in the pie plate from the refrigerator and pour the filling into it.

Step 7

In a small bowl, whisk the remaining egg and 1 tablespoon water to create an egg wash. Using a pastry brush, lightly brush the edges of the crust with the egg wash. Reserve the remaining egg wash.

Step 8

Bake for 10 minutes, then (without opening the oven) reduce the oven temperature to 350°F and bake for 30 to 35 minutes more, or until the center is set. Turn off the oven, crack open the oven door, and leave the pie in the oven for 10 to 15 minutes to adjust to the change in temperature.

Step 9

Transfer the pie to a wire rack and let it cool completely, at least 2 to 3 hours, before serving.

Step 10

While the pie cools, preheat the oven to 350°F. Line a baking sheet with parchment paper.

Step 11

Remove the second portion of rolled-out dough from the refrigerator. Using cookie cutters, make leaf or pumpkin shapes to decorate the pie. If the dough is too hard, let it sit a few minutes. Transfer the shapes to the clean prepared baking sheet and lightly brush them with the remaining egg wash.

Step 12

Bake for 10 minutes, or until golden.

Step 13

Let the shapes cool on the baking sheet for at least 10 minutes, then gently transfer to a wire rack to cool completely.

TO MAKE THE COCONUT WHIPPED CREAM

Step 14

Open the chilled can of coconut cream and pour off the watery liquid. Scoop only the solid part into a large bowl and add the powdered sugar. Using a handheld electric mixer, beat until smooth and fluffy.

Step 15

Place the cooled cutouts on top of the cooled pie. Slice and serve with a dollop of coconut whipped cream.

Step 16

Refrigerate leftover pie and whipped cream separately, covered, for up to 3 days.

Savory Tomato GaletteSnickerdoodle Apple Cobbler

MAKES 1 (9-BY-13-INCH) COBBLER

Prep time: 30 minutes
 Cook time: 35 minutes

Ingredients:

- Shortening, for preparing the pan

FOR THE SNICKERDOODLE TOPPING

- 190 grams All-Purpose Flour Blend

- 150 grams cane sugar or granulated sugar
- 1 teaspoon xanthan gum
- 1 teaspoon cream of tartar
- 1 teaspoon ground cinnamon
- ½ teaspoon baking soda
- ½ teaspoon salt
- 8 tablespoons (1 stick) butter or nondairy alternative
- 1 large egg

FOR THE CINNAMON SUGAR

- 2 tablespoons cane sugar or granulated sugar
- 1 teaspoon ground cinnamon

FOR THE FILLING

- 100 grams cane sugar or granulated sugar

- 32 grams All-Purpose Flour Blend

- ¼ teaspoon xanthan gum
- 1 teaspoon ground cinnamon
- 1,200 grams sliced peeled Granny Smith or Honeycrisp apples
- 1 tablespoon fresh lemon juice
- 1 teaspoon vanilla extract

Directions:

Step 1

Preheat the oven to 375°F. Grease a 9-by-13-inch pan with shortening.

TO MAKE THE SNICKERDOODLE TOPPING

Step 2

In a medium bowl, whisk the flour, sugar, xanthan gum, cream of tartar, cinnamon, baking soda, and salt to combine.

Step 3

Cut the butter into pieces and add it to the flour mixture along with the egg. Using a handheld electric mixer, mix the ingredients. The dough may seem dry and crumbly, but that is okay. Set aside.

TO MAKE THE CINNAMON SUGAR

Step 4

In a small bowl, stir together the sugar and cinnamon.

TO MAKE THE FILLING

Step 5

In a large bowl, whisk the sugar, flour, xanthan gum, and cinnamon to combine. Add the apples and, using a spatula, fold them into the flour mixture. Sprinkle the lemon juice and vanilla over the top and give it all another stir.

Step 6

Pour the apples evenly into the prepared pan. Using your clean hands, flatten pieces of snickerdoodle topping and place them over the apples as close together as possible to form a crust. Sprinkle the cinnamon sugar over the top.

Step 7

Bake for 20 minutes. Check that it is not browning too quickly. Loosely cover with aluminum foil, if needed, and bake for 15 minutes, or until the top is golden and the apples are bubbling.

Step 8

Serve warm. Refrigerate leftovers, covered, for up to 3 days. Reheat to serve.

Sliced Banana Bread Cobbler

MAKES 1 (9-BY-9-INCH) COBBLER

Prep time: 30 minutes
 Cook time: 40 minutes

Ingredients:

- Shortening, for preparing the pan

- 200 grams light brown sugar

- 32 grams All-Purpose Flour Blend

- ½ teaspoon ground cinnamon, plus more for sprinkling
- ¼ teaspoon xanthan gum
- 5 bananas, sliced
- 1 large egg, beaten
- 1 cup whole milk or coconut milk beverage
- 8 tablespoons (1 stick) butter or nondairy alternative, melted
- 6 or 7 slices Chocolate Chip Banana Bread , made without the chocolate chips

Directions:

Step 1

Preheat the oven to 350°F. Grease a 9-by-9-inch pan with shortening.

Step 2

In a large bowl, whisk the brown sugar, flour, cinnamon, and xanthan gum to combine. Add the bananas and stir to coat them well. Spread the bananas in the prepared pan. The pan should be about half full. Add or subtract pieces, if needed.

Step 3

In a small bowl, whisk the egg, milk, and melted butter until blended.

Step 4

Cut the crusts off the bread if desired, then cut each slice into thin strips. Lay the bread strips over the bananas.

Step 5

Pour the egg mixture over the top. Do not stir. Sprinkle lightly with cinnamon.

Step 6

Bake for 35 to 40 minutes, or until golden.

Step 7

Refrigerate leftovers in an airtight container for up to 3 days.

Easy Blackberry Cobbler

MAKES 1 (9-BY-13-INCH) COBBLER

Prep time: 10 minutes

 Cook time: about 1 hour

Ingredients:

- Shortening, for preparing the pan

- 250 grams cane sugar or granulated sugar, divided

- 125 grams All-Purpose Flour Blend

- 1½ teaspoons baking powder
- ½ teaspoon xanthan gum
- ½ teaspoon salt
- 1 cup whole milk or coconut milk beverage
- 4 tablespoons butter or nondairy alternative, melted
- ½ teaspoon apple cider vinegar
- 230 grams blackberries
- 2 tablespoons raw turbinado sugar

Directions:

Step 1

Preheat the oven to 350°F. Grease a 9-by-13-inch baking dish with shortening.

Step 2

In a medium bowl, whisk 200 grams of cane sugar, the flour, baking powder, xanthan gum, and salt to combine. Using a spatula, stir in the milk, melted butter, and vinegar, mixing just until combined.

Step 3

Pour the batter into the prepared baking dish. Arrange the blackberries on top so they are evenly distributed. They will sink into the dough as they bake. Sprinkle the remaining 50 grams of cane sugar over the blackberries.

Step 4

Bake for 50 minutes. Remove and sprinkle the turbinado sugar over the top. Return to the oven and bake for 10 minutes more, or until golden brown. Serve warm.

Step 5

Refrigerate leftover cobbler, covered, for up to 3 days. Reheat to serve.

The Easiest Baked Flatbread

MAKES 1 (10-INCH) FLATBREAD

Prep time: 15 minutes
 Cook time: 25 minutes

Ingredients:

- 62 grams Bread Flour Blend , plus more for dusting

- 2 teaspoons baking powder
- ½ teaspoon xanthan gum
- 120 grams plain Greek yogurt or nondairy alternative

- 1 tablespoon extra-virgin olive oil

Directions:

Step 1

Position an oven rack in the lower third of the oven. Place a cast-iron skillet or baking sheet in the oven to preheat, and set the oven to 375°F.

Step 2

Place a sheet of parchment paper on a work surface and lightly dust it with flour.

Step 3

In a medium bowl, whisk the flour, baking powder, and xanthan gum to combine. Using a wooden spoon or spatula, stir in the yogurt until a smooth dough ball forms.

Step 4

Transfer the dough to the floured parchment. Pour the olive oil into a small bowl. Dip your fingertips in the oil and flatten the dough into a 10-inch round about ¼ inch thick. Do not use a rolling pin. If the dough sticks to your fingertips, lightly dip them in the oil again. Lightly brush the remaining oil over the top of the flatbread.

Step 5

Trim the parchment paper so there is plenty of border around the flatbread and it will fit in the skillet. Using the parchment, transfer the flatbread to the preheated skillet or baking sheet.

Step 6

Bake for 10 minutes. Using a fork, lift one edge of the flatbread and remove the parchment. Bake directly in the pan or on the baking sheet for 10 to 15 minutes more, or until crisp. This is best served the same day.

Garlic and Herb Focaccia

MAKES 1 (9-INCH) FOCACCIA

Prep time: 2 hours 15 minutes
Cook time: 22 minutes

Ingredients:

- 8 tablespoons olive oil, divided, plus more for the baking dish and your fingertips

- 282 grams Bread Flour Blend

- 2 teaspoons xanthan gum
- 1 teaspoon baking powder
- 1½ teaspoons salt
- ¼ teaspoon garlic powder
- 2 teaspoons cane sugar or granulated sugar

- 1 (7-gram) packet instant (fast-acting) yeast
- 1 cup warm (100° to 110°F) water
- 2 garlic cloves, minced
- Fresh or dried herbs of choice, for topping
- Coarse sea salt
- Freshly ground black pepper

Directions:

Step 1

Lightly grease a 9-inch round glass baking dish with oil.

Step 2

In a medium bowl, whisk the flour, xanthan gum, baking powder, salt, and garlic powder to combine.

Step 3

In a large bowl, stir together the sugar, yeast, and warm water. Let stand for 5 minutes.

Step 4

Add 3 tablespoons of the oil and stir again. Using a handheld electric mixer fitted with the dough hook, add half the flour mixture to the yeast mixture, and mix on low speed to combine. Add the remaining flour and mix until a dough forms.

Step 5

Coat your fingertips in oil and transfer the dough to the prepared baking dish, spreading it evenly and folding down the edges. Cover tightly with plastic wrap and let rise for 1 hour, or until almost doubled in size.

Step 6

Using a spatula, gently lift each side of the bread while pouring 3 tablespoons of oil underneath the dough. Slide the dough around in the baking dish to distribute the oil. Re-cover the pan tightly with plastic and refrigerate for at least 1 hour.

Step 7

Preheat the oven to 450°F. Let the hot oven sit empty for at least 15 minutes at full temperature before baking.

Step 8

In a small bowl, whisk the remaining 2 tablespoons of oil, the garlic, and herbs to taste until blended. Season with salt and pepper and whisk to combine.

Step 9

Using your fingers, create dimples all over the surface of the dough. Using a pastry brush, brush the herb oil over the dough.

Step 10

Bake for 20 to 25 minutes, or until golden. If desired, broil the focaccia for 1 to 2 minutes to give it extra color and toast the garlic.

Step 11

Let the focaccia cool in the dish for 10 minutes before slicing and serving warm, or transfer to a wire rack to cool completely. Keep leftovers covered at room temperature for up to 2 days, or refrigerate for up to 1 week. Rewarm to serve.

Thin and Crispy Pizza Crust

MAKES 2 (10-INCH) CRUSTS

Prep time: 1 hour 20 minutes
Cook time: 25 minutes

Ingredients:

- 375 grams All-Purpose Flour Blend , plus more for dusting
- 2 tablespoons xanthan gum
- 1½ teaspoons salt
- 1 (7-gram) packet instant (fast-acting) yeast
- 1 tablespoon cane sugar or granulated sugar
- 1 cup (100° to 110°F) warm water
- ¼ cup olive oil, plus 1 tablespoon
- 1 large egg, beaten
- 1 tablespoon honey
- ½ teaspoon apple cider vinegar
- Pizza sauce, for topping
- Toppings of choice

Directions:

Step 1

Position an oven rack in the lower third of the oven. Place two sheets of parchment paper on a work surface and dust with flour.

Step 2

In a medium bowl, whisk the flour, xanthan gum, and salt to combine.

Step 3

In a large bowl, stir together the yeast, sugar, and warm water. Let sit for 5 minutes.

Step 4

Stir in ¼ cup of oil, the beaten egg, honey, and vinegar. Using a handheld electric mixer fitted with the dough attachment, add half the flour mixture and mix on low speed to combine. Add the remaining flour mixture and mix to form a dough.

Step 5

Pour the remaining 1 tablespoon of oil into a small bowl. Dip your fingertips in the oil and transfer the dough to the floured parchment. Divide the dough into 2 portions. (If only using one crust, see Tip.)

Step 6

Roll one portion of dough between the two sheets of parchment to about ⅛ inch thick. Use your hands to adjust the edges and create a nice round. Transfer the dough on the parchment to a pizza pan. If making a second crust, pull out another sheet of parchment paper and dust it with flour, then repeat the rolling process. Let the pizza round(s) rest and rise for at least 1 hour.

Step 7

Preheat the oven to 450°F.

Step 8

Bake one pizza crust for 5 minutes. Remove the crust from the oven and slide the parchment out from underneath, leaving the crust on the pan. Top as desired with sauce, cheese, and other toppings of choice. Bake for 15 to 20 minutes more, or until crisp. Repeat for a second pizza if making one.

Step 9

Let the pizza sit for 5 minutes before slicing. Refrigerate leftovers, covered, for up to 3 days.

Skillet Pizza Crust

MAKES 2 (12-INCH) CRUSTS
Prep time: 1 hour 50 minutes
 Cook time: 25 minutes

Ingredients:

- 375 grams All-Purpose Flour Blend , plus more for dusting

- 1 tablespoon xanthan gum
- 1½ teaspoons salt
- 1 (7-gram) packet instant (fast-acting) yeast
- ¼ cup olive oil, plus 2 tablespoons
- 1 large egg
- 1 tablespoon honey
- 1½ cups plus 2 tablespoons warm (100° to 110°F) water
- Pizza toppings, of choice

Directions:

Step 1

Position an oven rack in the lower third of the oven.

Step 2

Cut a piece of parchment paper to 14 inches. Fold it into fourths and round off the corners. Open the parchment into a round. Repeat to make one more parchment round.

Step 3

Place an additional piece of parchment on a work surface. Place one round on top and dust it with flour.

Step 4

In a medium bowl, whisk the flour, xanthan gum, salt, and yeast to combine.

Step 5

In a large bowl, using a handheld electric mixer, beat ¼ cup of oil, the egg, and honey, mixing until the egg is fully beaten. Add the warm water and mix for 1 minute. Add the flour mixture and mix until combined and a wet dough forms; it will look like batter. Using a spatula, fold the dough into a ball.

Step 6

Pour the remaining 2 tablespoons of oil into a small bowl. Coat your fingers and palms in about 1 tablespoon of the oil and swipe the edge of a bench scraper with oil as well. Using the bench scraper, cut down the middle of the dough and lift one half, transferring it to the flour-dusted parchment round.

Step 7

Using oiled hands, spread the dough from the middle outward into a 12-inch round. If the dough sticks to your fingers, dab them with more oil. Be careful not to flood the dough with too much oil. Slide the crust to the side using the parchment round.

Step 8

Place the second parchment round on your work surface and dust it with flour. Transfer the remaining dough to the parchment round and repeat step 7 with the remaining 1 tablespoon of oil. (If not baking 2 pizzas, shape and refrigerate the second crust for the next day.)

Step 9

Let the dough rest for 1 to 1½ hours.

Step 10

Preheat the oven to 425°F. Preheat a cast-iron skillet in the hot oven for at least 30 minutes.

Step 11

Transfer one crust, on the parchment round, to a pizza peel or rimless baking sheet and carefully slide the crust, still on the parchment, into the hot skillet.

Step 12

Bake for 5 minutes.

Step 13

Using oven mitts, remove the skillet from the oven and place it on a heat-resistant surface. Using the bench scraper, lift one edge of the crust and gently grab the parchment and remove it.

Step 14

Add any desired toppings to the pizza. Bake for 20 to 25 minutes more, or until the outer crust is golden and crisp.

Step 15

Remove from the oven, lift one edge of the pizza with a utensil, and slide it onto a tray or plate. Let the pizza cool for a few minutes before slicing and serving.

Step 16

If making the second pizza, repeat to bake and top as directed.

Pepperoni Pizza Rolls

MAKES 12 PIZZA ROLLS

Prep time: 1 hour 15 minutes
 Cook time: 30 minutes

Ingredients:

FOR THE CRUST

- 437 grams All-Purpose Flour Blend , plus more for dusting
- 2 teaspoons xanthan gum
- 1 teaspoon salt
- 1 tablespoon cane sugar or granulated sugar
- 1 (7-gram) packet instant (fast-acting) yeast
- 1⅓ cups (100° to 110°F) warm water
- 2 tablespoons olive oil
- ½ teaspoon apple cider vinegar

FOR THE FILLING

- ½ cup gluten-free pizza sauce
- 100 grams shredded mozzarella cheese or nondairy alternative, plus more for topping (optional)
- 1 (4-ounce) package sliced gluten-free pepperoni (I like Applegate brand), plus more diced for topping (optional)

Directions:

TO MAKE THE CRUST

Step 1

Position an oven rack in the lower third of the oven. Place two sheets of parchment paper on a work surface and dust them with flour.

Step 2

In a medium bowl, whisk the flour, xanthan gum, and salt to combine.

Step 3

In a large bowl, combine the sugar, yeast, and warm water. Give it a stir and let the mixture sit for 5 minutes.

Step 4

Add the oil and vinegar and give it another quick stir. Beat in the flour mixture in two additions and stir until a dough forms.

Step 5

Transfer the dough to the flour-dusted parchment and flatten it by hand. Place the second sheet of parchment on top and roll the dough to ⅛ to ¼ inch thick—the thinner, the better.

TO MAKE THE FILLING

Step 6

Line a baking sheet with parchment paper.

Step 7

Spread the pizza sauce evenly over the dough, leaving a ½-inch border. Cover with the cheese and arrange the pepperoni on top. Gently lift the edge closest to you and roll the pizza into a long log. Give it a gentle roll to seal the seam. Using a sharp knife, cut the roll into 12 pieces and place them on the prepared baking sheet. Cover loosely with plastic wrap and let them rest and rise for at least 1 hour.

Step 8

Preheat the oven to 475°F.

Step 9

Top the pizza rolls with more cheese (if using) and diced pepperoni (if using).

Step 10

Bake for 25 to 30 minutes, or until crisp.

Step 11

Let the rolls cool for about 5 minutes, then serve immediately. They are best served the same day. Refrigerate leftovers, covered, for up to 3 days. Reheat to serve.

Stromboli Pockets

MAKES 6 TO 8

Prep time: 1 hour 15 minutes
Cook time: 20 minutes

Ingredients:

FOR THE CRUST

- 375 grams All-Purpose Flour Blend , plus more for dusting

- 1 large egg
- 3 tablespoons olive oil, divided
- 2 teaspoons xanthan gum
- 1½ teaspoons salt
- 1 tablespoon cane sugar or granulated sugar
- 1 (7-gram) packet instant (fast-acting) yeast
- 1 cup warm (100° to 110°F) water
- 1 tablespoon honey
- ½ teaspoon apple cider vinegar

FOR THE POCKETS

- ¾ cup gluten-free pizza sauce
- 8 slices gluten-free salami
- 4 slices gluten-free deli ham
- 16 slices gluten-free pepperoni
- 100 grams shredded mozzarella cheese or nondairy alternative

Directions:

TO MAKE THE CRUST

Step 1

Position an oven rack in the lower third of the oven. Place two sheets of parchment paper on a work surface and dust them with flour. Line a baking sheet with parchment.

Step 2

In a small bowl, whisk the egg and 1 tablespoon water to create an egg wash. Pour 1 tablespoon of oil in another small bowl. Place the bowls next to the work surface.

Step 3

In a medium bowl, whisk the flour, xanthan gum, and salt to combine.

Step 4

In a large bowl, combine the sugar, yeast, and warm water. Give it a stir and let sit for 5 minutes.

Step 5

Add the remaining 2 tablespoons of oil, the honey, and vinegar and give it another quick stir. Stir in the flour mixture in two additions and stir until a dough forms.

Step 6

Transfer the dough to the floured work surface. Dip your fingertips in the oil bath and flatten the dough by hand. Divide it into 2 equal portions. Place the second sheet of parchment on top of one portion and roll the dough to ⅛ inch thick. You want this to be thin so the filling is prominent. Using a pizza cutter, cut the dough into 3 or 4 large pieces. The shape doesn't matter. Gather, reroll, and cut the scraps as you can. Repeat with the second portion of dough.

TO FILL THE POCKETS

Step 7

Spread about 1 tablespoon of pizza sauce in the middle of each piece. Evenly divide the salami, ham, pepperoni, and cheese between the dough pieces.

Step 8

Gently lift one edge of each piece and fold it over the filling to create a tube. Dip your finger in the egg wash and seal the seam. Push down the edges and seal both ends with some of the egg wash as well. (Reserve the remaining egg wash.) Using the tines of a fork, crimp the edges and transfer the stromboli pockets to the prepared baking sheet. Cover with plastic wrap and let them rest and rise for 30 to 60 minutes.

Step 9

Preheat the oven to 450°F.

Step 10

Using a pastry brush, brush each stromboli pocket with the reserved egg wash. Bake for 15 to 20 minutes, or until golden brown.

Step 11

Let the pockets cool on the baking sheet for 5 minutes and serve. Refrigerate leftovers, covered, for up to 2 days. Reheat to serve.

Sicilian Deep-Dish Pizza

MAKES 1 (9-BY-13-INCH) PIZZA

Prep time: 1 hour 15 minutes

 Cook time: 35 minutes

Ingredients:

FOR THE CRUST

- 437 grams Bread Flour Blend

- 1 (7-gram) packet instant (fast-acting) yeast
- 1 tablespoon xanthan gum
- 1 tablespoon salt
- 1 teaspoon cane sugar or granulated sugar
- 1½ cups warm (100° to 110°F) water
- 2 tablespoons extra-virgin olive oil, plus more for the pan and fingertips

FOR THE TOPPING

- 8 slices deli mozzarella cheese or nondairy alternative
- ½ cup gluten-free pizza sauce

- 1 (4-ounce) package sliced gluten-free pepperoni
- 1 ounce Parmesan cheese or nondairy alternative, grated

Directions:

TO MAKE THE CRUST

Step 1

In a large bowl, whisk the flour, yeast, xanthan gum, salt, and sugar to combine. Add the warm water and oil. Using a handheld electric mixer fitted with the dough attachment, mix on medium-high speed until a dough forms.

Step 2

Using a pastry brush (a paper towel is too absorbent and will soak up the oil), generously coat a 9-by-13-inch baking dish with oil, coating the bottom and sides. This will create a crispy crust.

Step 3

Oil your fingertips and transfer the dough into the prepared pan. Using your fingers, spread the dough evenly in the pan so it touches all the edges. Cover the dough with plastic wrap and a clean kitchen towel and let it rest for at least 1 hour.

TO MAKE THE TOPPING

Step 4

Preheat the oven to 450°F.

Step 5

Unwrap the pan and arrange the cheese slices on the dough, leaving a ½-inch border.

Step 6

Pour the pizza sauce in the center of the dough and use the back of a spoon to spread it all around. Add the pepperoni, overlapping, leaving a ½-inch border around the pizza, and sprinkle with Parmesan.

Step 7

Bake for 35 minutes, or until crisp.

Step 8

Run a butter knife along the edges of the pizza to loosen it from the pan. The pizza should come out easily. Cut and serve. Refrigerate leftovers, covered, for up to 2 days.

Everything Bagels

MAKES 8 BAGELS

Prep time: 1 hour 45 minutes

Cook time: 35 minutes

Ingredients:

FOR THE BAGELS

- 375 grams Bread Flour Blend , plus 32 grams
- 1 tablespoon light brown sugar
- 1 tablespoon xanthan gum
- 2 teaspoons baking powder
- 2 teaspoons salt
- 1 teaspoon cane sugar or granulated sugar
- 1 (7-gram) packet instant (fast-acting) yeast
- 1½ cups warm (100° to 110°F) water
- 1 large egg, beaten
- 1 tablespoon honey
- ½ teaspoon apple cider vinegar
- 1 tablespoon olive oil

FOR THE WATER BATH

- ¼ cup honey

FOR THE TOPPING

- 4 teaspoons dried minced garlic
- 4 teaspoons dried minced onion
- 4 teaspoons sesame seeds
- 2 teaspoons poppy seeds
- 2 teaspoons coarse sea salt
- ½ teaspoon freshly ground black pepper
- 1 large egg

Directions:

TO MAKE THE BAGELS

Step 1

Place two sheets of parchment paper on a work surface and place the 32 grams of flour in a corner. Dust a little flour onto one piece of parchment and save the rest.

Step 2

Line 2 baking sheets with parchment paper or silicone baking mats. Take an additional piece of parchment and fold it into eighths. Cut out 8 squares and place them on top of the prepared baking sheets.

Step 3

In a medium bowl, whisk the flour, brown sugar, xanthan gum, baking powder, and salt to combine.

Step 4

In a large bowl, combine the cane sugar, yeast, and 1 cup of warm water. Give it a quick stir and let sit for 5 minutes.

Step 5

Add the beaten egg, remaining ½ cup of warm water, honey, and vinegar. Stir again until combined. Using a handheld electric mixer fitted with the dough hook, add half the flour and mix on low speed to combine. Add the remaining flour and mix to form a dough. The dough will be sticky.

Step 6

Pour the oil into a small dish and dip your fingertips into it. Transfer the dough to the floured work surface. Add some of the remaining 32 grams of flour a little at a time to the dough. If the dough sticks to your fingers, dip them in oil. Repeat this process until the dough is not as sticky. Divide the dough into 8 portions.

Step 7

Roll each dough portion into a ball. Poke a hole through the middle with your finger and smooth the tops. Continue to dip your fingers in the oil if necessary but do not flood the dough with oil. Place each bagel on a parchment square. Cover loosely with plastic wrap and let the dough rest and rise for at least 1 hour.

Step 8

Position an oven rack in the lower third of the oven and preheat the oven to 425°F.

TO MAKE THE WATER BATH

Step 9

In a medium saucepan, stir together 2 quarts of water and honey. Bring to a boil over medium-high heat.

Step 10

Working in batches of 2 to 4 bagels, making sure they have room to move and float, pick each up using the parchment square and carefully drop into the boiling water. Cook for 1 minute, flip and cook for 1 minute more. Once finished, gently and carefully smooth the tops and fix the shape of each with your fingers. Transfer to a wire rack and repeat with the remaining bagels.

TO MAKE THE TOPPING

Step 11

In a shallow bowl, stir together the garlic, onion, sesame seeds, poppy seeds, coarse sea salt, and pepper.

Step 12

In a small bowl, whisk the egg with 1 tablespoon water to create an egg wash. Using a pastry brush, brush the egg wash over the top and sides of each bagel. Dip each coated bagel in the spice topping, turning to coat all sides. Transfer to the prepared baking sheets, 4 bagels per sheet.

Step 13

Bake for 25 to 30 minutes until golden brown.

Step 14

Let the bagels cool for 10 minutes on the baking sheet, then transfer them to a wire rack to cool completely. Tightly wrap and store leftovers in an airtight container at room temperature for up to 3 days or freeze for up to 1 month.

Soft Pretzels

MAKES 4 PRETZELS

Prep time: 2 hours 20 minutes

Cook time: 30 minutes

Ingredients:

- 62 grams All-Purpose Flour Blend , plus more for dusting

- 190 grams Bread Flour Blend

- 1 (7-gram) packet instant (fast-acting) yeast
- 1 tablespoon light brown sugar
- 1½ teaspoons xanthan gum
- 1 teaspoon salt
- 2 large eggs, divided
- ¼ cup sparkling water
- ½ teaspoon apple cider vinegar
- ½ cup warm (100° to 110°F) whole milk or coconut milk beverage
- 1½ teaspoons olive oil
- 2 tablespoons baking soda
- Coarse sea salt

Directions:

Step 1

Line a baking sheet with parchment paper. Place another large sheet of parchment on a clean work surface and dust it with all-purpose flour.

Step 2

In a medium bowl, whisk the all-purpose flour, bread flour, yeast, brown sugar, xanthan gum, and salt to combine.

Step 3

In a large bowl, using a handheld electric mixer, beat 1 egg, the sparkling water, and vinegar. Change to a dough hook and add the flour mixture, mixing on low speed. Add the warm milk and mix to form a dough.

Step 4

Transfer the dough to the floured work surface and dust it with flour to prevent sticking. Shape the dough into an 8-inch log. Cut the log into 4 (2-inch) portions.

Step 5

Pour the oil into a small bowl. Dip your fingertips into the oil and, using your hands, roll one portion into a rope about 12 to 14 inches long. Shape it into a pretzel by bringing the two ends toward you to form a horseshoe shape. Wrap one end over the other and bring the bottom piece around the top piece to form a twist (the ends should still be separate). Bring the ends to the dough ring and press them in to secure. Place on the prepared baking sheet. Repeat with the remaining portions. Cover loosely with plastic wrap and let them rest for at least 2 hours.

Step 6

Preheat the oven to 425°F.

Step 7

In a small saucepan, combine 3 cups water and the baking soda and bring to a boil. Use your finger to smooth out any holes or lumps that have appeared on the dough, and make sure the ends are sealed. One at a time, place each pretzel in the boiling water, front-side down. Boil for 30 seconds per side. The pretzels are delicate, so handle them using 2 forks or a slotted spatula. Transfer the boiled pretzel to the prepared baking sheet.

Step 8

In a small bowl, whisk the remaining egg with 1 tablespoon water to create an egg wash. Using a pastry brush, brush a light layer of egg wash on each pretzel. Sprinkle coarse sea salt over the top.

Step 9

Bake for 20 minutes until the pretzels are golden brown.

Step 10

Let the pretezels cool for 5 minutes on the baking sheet and serve warm, or transfer to a wire rack to cool completely. The pretzels are best eaten the same day.

Garlic Butter Breadsticks

MAKES 8 BREADSTICKS

Prep time: 2 hours 15 minutes

 Cook time: 15 minutes

Ingredients:

FOR THE BREADSTICKS

190 grams Bread Flour Blend

2 tablespoons cane sugar or granulated sugar, divided

1 teaspoon salt

1 teaspoon xanthan gum

½ teaspoon baking powder

1½ tablespoons olive oil

¼ teaspoon garlic powder

1 teaspoon instant (fast-acting) yeast

¾ cup warm (100° 110°F) water

½ teaspoon apple cider vinegar

FOR THE GARLIC BUTTER

2 tablespoons butter or nondairy alternative

½ teaspoon garlic powder

Directions:

TO MAKE THE BREADSTICKS

Step 1

Line a baking sheet with parchment paper or a silicone baking mat.

Step 2

In a medium bowl, whisk the flour, 1 tablespoon of sugar, the salt, xanthan gum, and baking powder to combine.

Step 3

In a small bowl, stir together the oil and garlic powder.

Step 4

In a large bowl, stir together the yeast, remaining 1 tablespoon of sugar, and warm water. Let sit for 5 minutes.

Step 5

Add the garlic oil and vinegar and give it a quick stir. Using a handheld electric mixer fitted with the dough attachment, or your clean hands, add half the flour mixture to the wet ingredients and mix on low speed to combine. Add the remaining flour mixture and mix to form a dough. It will be sticky.

Step 6

Transfer the dough to a piping bag or plastic bag and cut the tip to about a 1-inch width. Squeeze the dough into 6-inch ropes onto the prepared baking sheet. Cover loosely with plastic wrap and let the dough rest and rise for at least 2 hours.

TO MAKE THE GARLIC BUTTER

Step 7

In a small saucepan, melt the butter over low heat. Stir in the garlic powder and cook, stirring, until the garlic powder dissolves.

Step 8

Position an oven rack in the lower third of the oven and preheat the oven to 425°F.

Step 9

Using a pastry brush, brush the breadsticks with some of the garlic butter. Reserve the remainder.

Step 10

Bake for 15 minutes, or until slightly golden.

Step 11

Remove from the oven and brush the breadsticks with the reserved garlic butter. Let the breadsticks cool on the baking sheet for 10 minutes.

Step 12

Serve warm or cool. Best served same day. Keep leftovers in an airtight container at room temperature for up to 3 days, or freeze for up to 1 month. Rewarm to serve.

Perfect Skillet Pancakes

MAKES 6 PANCAKES

Prep time: 10 minutes

Cook time: 20 minutes

Ingredients:

- Butter, for greasing the skillet

- 125 grams All-Purpose Flour Blend

- 2 tablespoons cane sugar or granulated sugar
- 1½ teaspoons baking powder
- ½ teaspoon salt
- ¼ teaspoon xanthan gum
- ¼ teaspoon baking soda
- ¾ cup whole milk or coconut milk beverage
- 1 large egg
- 2 tablespoons avocado oil or canola oil
- Maple syrup, for serving

Directions:

Step 1

Heat a skillet over low heat. Cut off a chunk of stick butter long enough to hold on to and have it at the ready.

Step 2

In a medium bowl, whisk the flour, sugar, baking powder, salt, xanthan gum, and baking soda to combine. Add the milk, egg, and oil. Mix to blend. Let the batter sit for 5 minutes.

Step 3

Hold the chunk of butter and use it to grease the skillet, spreading it all around the skillet as you increase the heat to medium. Pour ¼ cup of batter into the skillet. Cook for about 3 minutes, or until bubbles form and begin to pop. Flip the pancake to the other side and cook for 2 to 3 minutes more, until set. The pancakes take less time to cook on the second side. Rub each pancake with butter and watch it melt into the pancake. Repeat with the remaining pancake batter, using more butter to grease the skillet as necessary.

Step 4

Drizzle maple syrup on top to serve. These are best served warm immediately.

Mom's French Toast

MAKES 6 SLICES

Prep time: 15 minutes
 Cook time: 25 minutes

Ingredients:

- 100 grams light brown sugar

- 1 teaspoon ground cinnamon
- 8 tablespoons (1 stick) butter or nondairy alternative, melted and slightly cooled
- 2 large eggs, beaten
- 1 cup whole milk or coconut milk beverage
- 2 tablespoons maple syrup, plus more for serving
- 1 tablespoon vanilla extract
- 6 slices gluten-free Sandwich Bread
- Gluten-free cooking spray
- Powdered sugar, for dusting

Directions:

Step 1

In a medium bowl, combine the brown sugar, cinnamon, melted butter, eggs, milk, maple syrup, and vanilla, in that order, and whisk to blend. Pour the mixture into a 9-by-13-inch baking pan. Add the bread slices and let sit for 1 to 2 minutes. Flip and let sit for 1 to 2 minutes more. Be careful not to let them sit too long or the bread will become soggy and break.

Step 2

Heat a skillet over medium heat. Coat the skillet with cooking spray. Place 1 slice of bread in the skillet and cook for about 3 minutes, or until the bottom seems to crisp up. Flip and cook for 2 to 3 minutes more. Repeat with the remaining slices.

Step 3

Dust the toast with powdered sugar and drizzle with maple syrup.

Overnight Waffles

MAKES 8 WAFFLES

Prep time: 10 minutes, plus overnight to chill

 Cook time: 20 minutes

Ingredients:

- 250 grams All-Purpose Flour Blend

- 1 tablespoon baking powder
- 1 teaspoon salt
- ½ teaspoon xanthan gum
- ½ teaspoon ground cinnamon
- 1 cup whole milk or coconut milk beverage
- 2 large eggs
- 6 tablespoons maple syrup, plus more for serving
- 4 tablespoons melted butter or nondairy alternative, cooled slightly, plus more for serving
- 1 teaspoon vanilla extract
- ½ teaspoon apple cider vinegar
- Gluten-free cooking spray

Directions:

Step 1

In a medium bowl, whisk the flour, baking powder, salt, xanthan gum, and cinnamon to combine.

Step 2

In a small bowl, whisk the milk, eggs, maple syrup, melted butter, vanilla, and vinegar.

Step 3

Make a small well in the middle of the flour mixture and add the egg mixture. Mix well. Cover the bowl and refrigerate overnight.

Step 4

Preheat a waffle iron according to the manufacturer's instructions. Coat it with cooking spray. Place ¼ cup of batter in the middle of the waffle iron and cook according to the manufacturer's instructions.

Step 5

Top with butter and drizzle with maple syrup.

Glazed Lemon Poppy Seed Loaf

MAKES 1 (9-BY-5-INCH) LOAF

Prep time: 20 minutes

Cook time: about 1 hour

Ingredients:

FOR THE BREAD

- Gluten-free cooking spray
- 375 grams All-Purpose Flour Blend
- 1 tablespoon poppy seeds
- 1½ teaspoons baking powder
- 1½ teaspoons xanthan gum
- ¾ teaspoon salt
- ½ teaspoon baking soda
- 100 grams cane sugar or granulated sugar
- 100 grams light brown sugar
- 3 large eggs
- ½ cup avocado oil or canola oil
- ⅔ cup cold water
- 2 tablespoons grated lemon zest
- 2 tablespoons fresh lemon juice
- 2 teaspoons vanilla extract

FOR THE LEMON GLAZE

- 210 grams powdered sugar
- 2 tablespoons grated lemon zest
- 2 tablespoons fresh lemon juice

Directions:

TO MAKE THE BREAD

Step 1

Preheat the oven to 350°F. Coat a 9-by-5-inch loaf pan with cooking spray or line it with parchment paper.

Step 2

In a medium bowl, whisk the flour, poppy seeds, baking powder, xanthan gum, salt, and baking soda to combine.

Step 3

In a large bowl, using a handheld electric mixer, beat the cane sugar, brown sugar, eggs, oil, cold water, lemon zest, lemon juice, and vanilla for 2 minutes. Add the flour mixture and beat until combined. Do not overmix. Pour the batter into the prepared loaf pan.

Step 4

Bake for 50 to 60 minutes, or until a toothpick inserted into the center of the loaf comes out clean.

Step 5

Let the loaf cool in the pan for 15 minutes, then gently remove the loaf and transfer it to a wire rack to cool completely.

TO MAKE THE LEMON GLAZE

Step 6

While the loaf cools, in a medium bowl, stir together the powdered sugar, lemon zest, and lemon juice until smooth.

Step 7

Pour the glaze over the cooled loaf. Tightly wrap any remaining bread and keep it at room temperature for up to 3 days, or refrigerate for up to 1 week.

Cinnamon Swirl Loaf

MAKES 1 (9-BY-5-INCH) LOAF

Prep time: 20 minutes
 Cook time: about 50 minutes

Ingredients:

FOR THE TOPPING

- 1 tablespoon light brown sugar
- 1 tablespoon cane sugar or granulated sugar
- 1 teaspoon ground cinnamon

FOR THE FILLING

- 2 tablespoons butter or nondairy alternative, melted
- 50 grams light brown sugar
- 2 tablespoons All-Purpose Flour Blend
- 1 tablespoon ground cinnamon

FOR THE LOAF

- Gluten-free cooking spray
- 250 grams All-Purpose Flour Blend
- 100 grams cane sugar or granulated sugar
- 100 grams light brown sugar
- 1 teaspoon xanthan gum
- 1 teaspoon baking powder
- ½ teaspoon baking soda

- ¼ teaspoon salt
- 1 cup buttermilk, or 1 cup coconut milk beverage plus 1 tablespoon apple cider vinegar (see here)
- 2 large eggs
- ¼ cup avocado oil or canola oil
- 2 teaspoons vanilla extract

Directions:

TO MAKE THE TOPPING

Step 1

In a small bowl, stir together the brown sugar, cane sugar, and cinnamon until blended.

TO MAKE THE FILLING

Step 2

In another small bowl, stir together the melted butter, brown sugar, flour, and cinnamon until combined.

TO MAKE THE LOAF

Step 3

Preheat the oven to 350°F. Coat a 9-by-5-inch loaf pan with cooking spray or line it with parchment paper.

Step 4

In a medium bowl, whisk the flour, cane sugar, brown sugar, xanthan gum, baking powder, baking soda, and salt to combine.

Step 5

In a large bowl, using a handheld electric mixer, beat the buttermilk, eggs, oil, and vanilla for 2 minutes. Add the flour mixture and beat until combined. Do not overmix.

Step 6

Pour half the batter into the prepared loaf pan. Drizzle the filling evenly on top. Pour the remaining batter over the filling. Using a butter knife, cut an "S" shape down the length of the pan to create the swirl. Finish by sprinkling the topping over the loaf.

Step 7

Bake for 45 to 50 minutes, or until a toothpick inserted into the center of the loaf comes out clean.

Step 8

Let the loaf cool in the pan for 15 minutes, then gently remove it and transfer to a wire rack to cool completely. Keep any remaining slices covered at room temperature for up to 3 days, or refrigerate for up to 5 days.

Double-Chocolate Zucchini Bread

MAKES 1 (9-BY-5-INCH) LOAF

Prep time: 25 minutes

Cook time: 50 minutes

Ingredients:

- Gluten-free cooking spray
- 225 grams grated zucchini
- 125 grams All-Purpose Flour Blend
- 50 grams all-natural unsweetened cocoa powder (not Dutch-process)
- 1 teaspoon xanthan gum
- ¾ teaspoon baking soda
- ¼ teaspoon baking powder
- ¼ teaspoon salt
- ½ teaspoon ground espresso
- 135 grams chocolate chips or nondairy alternative
- 100 grams cane sugar or granulated sugar
- 2 large eggs
- ¼ cup avocado oil or canola oil
- 60 grams vanilla Greek yogurt or nondairy alternative
- 1 teaspoon vanilla extract

Directions:

Step 1

Preheat the oven to 350°F. Coat a 9-by-5-inch loaf pan with cooking spray or line it with parchment paper.

Step 2

Place the zucchini between 2 paper towels to absorb most of the moisture.

Step 3

In a medium bowl, whisk the flour, cocoa powder, xanthan gum, baking soda, baking powder, salt, espresso, and chocolate chips.

Step 4

In a small bowl, whisk the sugar, eggs, oil, yogurt, and vanilla. Using a spatula, add the flour mixture and mix until combined. Do not overmix. Fold in the zucchini. Pour this thick batter into the prepared loaf pan.

Step 5

Bake for 45 to 50 minutes, or until a toothpick inserted into the center of the loaf comes out clean. This bread could take a little longer to cook.

Step 6

Let the bread cool in the pan for at least 15 minutes. Gently remove from the pan and transfer the bread to a wire rack to cool completely. Store leftovers in an airtight container at room temperature for up to 5 days, or freeze to enjoy a slice whenever you desire. Let each slice thaw naturally.

Chocolate Chip Banana Bread

MAKES 1 (9-BY-5-INCH) LOAF

Prep time: 15 minutes

 Cook time: about 1 hour

Ingredients:

- Shortening or gluten-free cooking spray, for preparing the pan

- 250 grams All-Purpose Flour Blend

- 1 teaspoon ground cinnamon
- 1 teaspoon xanthan gum
- 1 teaspoon baking powder
- ½ teaspoon baking soda
- ¼ teaspoon salt
- 8 tablespoons (1 stick) butter or nondairy alternative
- 150 grams light brown sugar
- 2 large eggs
- 80 grams plain Greek yogurt or nondairy alternative
- 450 grams mashed bananas (about 4 large bananas)
- 1 teaspoon vanilla extract
- 90 grams mini semisweet chocolate chips or nondairy alternative

Directions:

Step 1

Preheat the oven to 350°F. Grease a 9-by-5-inch loaf pan with shortening or gluten-free cooking spray.

Step 2

In a medium bowl, whisk the flour, cinnamon, xanthan gum, baking powder, baking soda, and salt to combine.

Step 3

In a large bowl, using a handheld electric mixer on medium speed, cream together the butter and brown sugar. Add the eggs and mix well, stopping to scrape down the bowl, as needed. Add the yogurt, bananas, and vanilla and mix well.

Step 4

Add half the flour mixture, reduce the mixer speed, and mix to combine. Add the remaining flour mixture and mix just until the batter is combined. Do not overmix. Using a rubber spatula, fold in the chocolate chips. Pour the batter into the prepared loaf pan.

Step 5

Bake for 1 hour, or until a toothpick inserted into the center of the bread comes out clean.

Step 6

Let the bread cool in the pan for at least 20 minutes, then gently transfer it to a wire rack to cool completely.

Cinnamon Roll PancakesBlondies

MAKES 12 BLONDIES

Prep time: 10 minutes
Cook time: 25 minutes

Ingredients:

- 125 grams All-Purpose Flour Blend

- 1 teaspoon ground cinnamon
- ½ teaspoon baking powder
- ½ teaspoon xanthan gum
- ¼ teaspoon salt
- ⅛ teaspoon baking soda
- 200 grams light brown sugar
- 5 tablespoons butter or nondairy alternative, melted
- 1 tablespoon vanilla extract
- 1 large egg

Directions:

Step 1

Preheat the oven to 350°F. Line a 9-by-9-inch baking pan with parchment paper, leaving some hanging over each side. This will make the cooked blondies easy to remove.

Step 2

In a medium bowl, whisk the flour, cinnamon, baking powder, xanthan gum, salt, and baking soda.

Step 3

In a large bowl, using a whisk or handheld electric mixer, mix the brown sugar, melted butter, and vanilla until well combined. Add the egg and mix again. Using a spatula, slowly add the flour mixture to the wet ingredients and stir just until combined. The batter will be very thick. Spread the batter evenly in the prepared pan, using the spatula and your fingertips to fill in the corners.

Step 4

Bake for 25 minutes, or until a toothpick inserted into the center of the blondies comes out clean.

Step 5

Let the blondies cool completely before cutting. Keep covered at room temperature for up to 5 days.

Chewy Fudgy Brownies

MAKES 16 BROWNIES

Prep time: 10 minutes

Cook time: 32 minutes

Ingredients:

- Gluten-free cooking spray
- 93 grams All-Purpose Flour Blend
- 150 grams cane sugar or granulated sugar
- 50 grams light brown sugar
- 25 grams Dutch-process cocoa powder
- ½ teaspoon xanthan gum
- ¼ teaspoon ground espresso
- ¼ teaspoon salt
- 8 tablespoons (1 stick) butter or nondairy alternative, melted
- 180 grams semisweet chocolate chips or nondairy alternative
- 3 large eggs
- 1 teaspoon vanilla extract

Directions:

Step 1

Preheat the oven to 350°F. Coat a 9-by-9-inch baking pan with cooking spray or line it with parchment paper, leaving some hanging over the edges for easy removal from the pan.

Step 2

In a medium bowl, whisk the flour, cane sugar, brown sugar, cocoa powder, xanthan gum, espresso, and salt to combine.

Step 3

In a small saucepan, melt the butter over low heat. Remove the pan from the heat and stir in the chocolate chips until smooth and melted. Transfer the mixture to a medium bowl and let it cool for 10 minutes. Add the eggs and vanilla and whisk well.

Step 4

Using a spatula, fold the flour mixture into the chocolate mixture just until combined. Transfer the batter to the prepared baking pan and spread it evenly. This batter will be thick.

Step 5

Bake for 30 to 32 minutes, or until a toothpick inserted into the center of the brownies comes out clean.

Step 6

Let the brownies cool before cutting them into squares. Keep covered at room temperature for up to 4 days.

Salted Caramel Brownies

MAKES 16 BROWNIES

Prep time: 30 minutes

Cook time: 50 minutes

Ingredients:

FOR THE BROWNIES

- Gluten-free cooking spray

- 93 grams All-Purpose Flour Blend

- 150 grams cane sugar or granulated sugar
- 50 grams light brown sugar
- 25 grams Dutch-process cocoa powder
- ½ teaspoon xanthan gum
- ¼ teaspoon salt
- 8 tablespoons (1 stick) butter or nondairy alternative
- 180 grams semisweet chocolate chips or nondairy alternative
- 3 large eggs
- 1 teaspoon vanilla extract

FOR THE SALTED CARAMEL SAUCE

- 200 grams cane sugar or granulated sugar
- 6 tablespoons butter or nondairy alternative
- ½ cup heavy cream or coconut cream
- 1 teaspoon salt

Directions:

TO MAKE THE BROWNIES

Step 1

Preheat the oven to 350°F. Coat a 9-by-9-inch baking pan with cooking spray or line it with parchment paper, leaving some hanging over the sides. This will make the brownies easy to remove.

Step 2

In a small bowl, whisk the flour, cane sugar, brown sugar, cocoa powder, xanthan gum, and salt to combine.

Step 3

In a small saucepan, melt the butter over low heat. Remove from the heat and stir in the chocolate chips until they are melted and smooth. Transfer the mixture to a large bowl and let it cool for 10 minutes.

Step 4

Add the eggs and vanilla to the chocolate mixture and, using a whisk or handheld electric mixer, mix well to combine.

Step 5

Using a spatula, fold in the flour mixture just until combined. This batter will be thick. Transfer the batter to the prepared baking pan and spread it evenly.

Step 6

Bake for 30 to 32 minutes, or until a toothpick inserted into the center of the brownies comes out clean.

Step 7

Let the brownies cool.

TO MAKE THE SALTED CARAMEL SAUCE

Step 8

In a small saucepan, melt the cane sugar over medium heat, stirring constantly. If your sugar is not melting, increase the heat just a bit. Keep stirring so the sugar does not burn (this can happen quickly).

Step 9

Once the sugar begins to melt, reduce the heat. Keep stirring until the sugar is completely melted. Remove the pan from the heat and slowly add the butter, being careful not to splatter hot sugar everywhere. Keep stirring as the butter melts.

Step 10

Slowly stir in the cream. Place the pan over medium-low heat. When everything is melted together, increase the heat and bring the mixture to a boil. Boil for 1 to 2 minutes, until slightly thickened. Remove the saucepan from the heat giving it one or two more stirs. Stir in the salt.

Step 11

Gently pour as much or as little of the caramel sauce as you want over the brownies. Let set for 5 minutes or more.

Step 12

Slice and serve the brownies. Keep the brownies covered at room temperature for up to 2 days. If the caramel melts because of humidity, refrigerate the brownies. If there is caramel sauce left, let it cool (it will thicken as it cools), transfer to an airtight glass container, and refrigerate for up to 1 month.

Pumpkin Everything Squares

MAKES 16 SQUARES

Prep time: 20 minutes
 Cook time: 45 minutes

Ingredients:

FOR THE GRAHAM CRACKER CRUST

- 130 grams gluten-free graham cracker crumbs, store-bought or homemade (here)
- 60 grams pumpkin seeds, chopped
- 2 tablespoons cane sugar or granulated sugar
- 8 tablespoons (1 stick) butter or nondairy alternative, melted and slightly cooled

FOR THE FILLING

- 32 grams All-Purpose Flour Blend

- 1½ teaspoons pumpkin pie spice
- 1 teaspoon ground cinnamon
- ¼ teaspoon xanthan gum
- ¼ teaspoon salt
- 1 (8-ounce) package cream cheese or nondairy alternative
- 1 (15-ounce) can pumpkin puree
- 200 grams light brown sugar
- 2 large eggs
- 1¼ cups whole milk or coconut milk beverage
- 2 teaspoons vanilla extract

Directions:

TO MAKE THE GRAHAM CRACKER CRUST

Step 1

Preheat the oven to 350°F. Line a 9-by-9-inch baking pan with parchment paper, leaving some hanging over the sides. This will make the bars easy to remove.

Step 2

In a food processor, combine the graham cracker crumbs, pumpkin seeds, and cane sugar. Pulse until a sandy consistency forms. With the processor running, slowly add the melted butter through the feed tube and watch the mixture thicken.

Step 3

Press this crust mixture firmly into the bottom of the prepared pan.

Step 4

Bake for 8 minutes. Remove the crust and leave the oven on.

TO MAKE THE FILLING

Step 5

In a small bowl, whisk the flour, pumpkin pie spice, cinnamon, xanthan gum, and salt to combine.

Step 6

In a large bowl, using a handheld electric mixer, beat the cream cheese until smooth and creamy. Add the pumpkin, brown sugar, eggs, milk, and vanilla and mix until combined. Add the flour mixture and mix until smooth. Do not overmix.

Step 7

Pour the filling into the graham cracker crust.

Step 8

Bake for 40 to 50 minutes, or until the center is set and doesn't jiggle.

Step 9

Let the squares cool completely on a wire rack. Once cooled, cover the pan with aluminum foil and refrigerate for at least 1 hour before slicing and serving. Keep refrigerated, covered, for up to 5 days.

Coconut Macaroons

MAKES 18 MACAROONS

Prep time: 45 minutes

Cook time: 15 minutes per batch

Ingredients:

- 42 grams All-Purpose Flour Blend

- ¼ teaspoon xanthan gum
- ¼ teaspoon salt
- 1 (**Step 7**4-ounce) can sweetened condensed coconut milk
- ½ teaspoon orange extract or almond extract
- 1 teaspoon vanilla extract
- 1 large egg white, beaten
- 100 grams unsweetened coconut flakes

Directions:

Step 1

In a small bowl, whisk the flour, xanthan gum, and salt to combine.

Step 2

In a medium bowl, whisk the condensed milk and extracts. Add the beaten egg white and whisk to combine. Stir in the flour mixture and coconut flakes, mixing well. Cover the bowl with plastic wrap and refrigerate for 30 minutes.

Step 3

Preheat the oven to 350°F. Line 2 baking sheets with parchment paper or silicone baking mats.

Step 4

Using a 1-inch ice cream scoop, scoop the macaroons onto the prepared baking sheets. Smooth the bottom edges.

Step 5

Baking one batch at a time, bake for 12 to 15 minutes, or until the coconut looks slightly toasted.

Step 6

Let the cookies cool on the pan for at least 10 minutes, then gently transfer to a wire rack to cool completely. Keep covered and at room temperature for up to 5 days.

Zesty Lemon Squares

MAKES 9 SQUARES

Prep time: 25 minutes

 Cook time: 45 minutes

Ingredients:

FOR THE CRUST

- 190 grams All-Purpose Flour Blend
- ½ teaspoon xanthan gum
- ½ teaspoon salt
- 12 tablespoons (1½ sticks) butter or nondairy alternative, melted and slightly cooled
- 100 grams cane sugar or granulated sugar
- 1 teaspoon vanilla extract

FOR THE FILLING

- 2 large eggs
- 200 grams cane sugar or granulated sugar
- 62 grams All-Purpose Flour Blend
- ½ teaspoon baking powder
- ¼ teaspoon xanthan gum
- ¼ teaspoon salt
- 1 tablespoon grated lemon zest (about 1 large lemon)
- ½ cup fresh lemon juice (about 3 large lemons)
- 3 tablespoons powdered sugar

Directions:

TO MAKE THE CRUST

Step 1

Preheat the oven to 350°F. Line a 9-by-9-inch baking pan with parchment paper, leaving some hanging over the edges. This will make the bars easy to remove.

Step 2

In a medium bowl, whisk the flour, xanthan gum, and salt to combine. Using a spatula, stir in the melted butter, sugar, and vanilla. Pour the crust into the prepared baking pan and spread it evenly.

Step 3

Bake for 20 minutes. Remove and leave the oven on.

TO MAKE THE FILLING

Step 4

While the crust bakes, in a small bowl, using a handheld electric mixer, beat the eggs.

Step 5

In a medium bowl, whisk the sugar, flour, baking powder, xanthan gum, and salt to combine. Add the beaten eggs, lemon zest, and lemon juice and mix well.

Step 6

Pour the filling evenly over the crust, then return to the oven and bake for 20 to 25 minutes, or until the middle is set and does not jiggle.

Step 7

Let the bars cool for 10 to 20 minutes, then cover with aluminum foil and refrigerate at least 1 hour.

Step 8

Dust the squares with the powdered sugar before serving. Refrigerate the bars, covered, for up to 5 days.

Red Velvet Whoopie Pies

MAKES 14 SANDWICH COOKIES

Prep time: 2 hours 35 minutes

Cook time: 12 minutes

Ingredients:

FOR THE PIES

- 250 grams All-Purpose Flour Blend

- 15 grams unsweetened natural cocoa powder
- 1 teaspoon baking soda
- ½ teaspoon xanthan gum
- ½ teaspoon salt

- 8 tablespoons (1 stick) butter or nondairy alternative
- 200 grams light brown sugar
- 1 large egg
- ⅔ cup whole milk or coconut milk beverage
- 2 teaspoons vanilla extract
- ½ teaspoon apple cider vinegar
- 1 teaspoon red gel food coloring

FOR THE FILLING

- 51 grams shortening
- 4 ounces cream cheese or nondairy alternative
- 1 tablespoon whole milk or coconut milk beverage
- 1 teaspoon vanilla extract
- 300 grams powdered sugar

Directions:

TO MAKE THE PIES

Step 1

In a medium bowl, whisk the flour, cocoa powder, baking soda, xanthan gum, and salt to combine.

Step 2

In a large bowl, using a handheld electric mixer on medium speed, cream the butter. Add the brown sugar and mix until well combined. Add the egg and mix well again. Add the milk, vanilla, and vinegar and mix again. The mixture will look curdled. That's okay.

Step 3

Add half the flour mixture and mix to combine. Add the remaining flour mixture and mix again. Add the red food coloring and mix until completely incorporated.

Step 4

Refrigerate for 2 hours to set, until the mixture looks like thick cupcake batter. During the last few minutes of chilling, preheat the oven to 350°F and line 2 baking sheets with parchment paper. (Don't use silicone mats because they might stain.)

Step 5

Using a 1-inch ice cream scoop, transfer tablespoon-size mounds of the batter onto the prepared baking sheets about 3 inches apart.

Step 6

Bake for 10 to 12 minutes until the centers appear set but the cookies are still soft. Cool for 10 minutes on the baking sheets, then gently transfer to a wire rack to cool completely.

TO MAKE THE FILLING

Step 7

In a medium bowl, using a handheld electric mixer on medium speed, cream together the shortening and cream cheese until smooth and creamy. Add the milk and vanilla. Mix, then add the powdered sugar and mix well until smooth.

Step 8

Pair the red velvet cookies by size. Spread a generous layer of filling on the inside of one cookie and top it with the other to form a sandwich. Repeat with the remaining cookies.

Step 9

Keep in an airtight container at room temperature for up to 3 days, or refrigerate for up to 5 days.

S'mores Cookies

MAKES 12 COOKIES

Prep time: 30 minutes

 Cook time: 18 minutes per batch

Ingredients:

- 50 grams mini marshmallows

- 250 grams All-Purpose Flour Blend

- 52 grams finely crushed Homemade Graham Crackers or gluten-free graham cracker crumbs
- 2 teaspoons arrowroot
- 1 teaspoon baking soda
- ½ teaspoon xanthan gum
- ½ teaspoon salt
- 8 tablespoons (1 stick) butter or nondairy alternative
- 150 grams light brown sugar
- 50 grams cane sugar or granulated sugar
- 1 large egg
- 2 teaspoons vanilla extract
- 180 grams semisweet chocolate chips or nondairy alternative

Directions:

Step 1

Preheat the oven to 375°F. Line 2 baking sheets with parchment paper or silicone baking mats.

Step 2

Cut the mini marshmallows in half using kitchen shears.

Step 3

In a medium bowl, whisk the flour, graham cracker crumbs, arrowroot, baking soda, xanthan gum, and salt to combine.

Step 4

In a large bowl, using a handheld electric mixer on medium speed, cream together the butter, brown sugar, and cane sugar. Add the egg and vanilla. Mix well to combine. Beat in the flour mixture in two additions and mix to form a dough. Using a spatula, fold in half the marshmallows and half the chocolate chips. The batter will be thick and sticky.

Step 5

Using tablespoon-size portions, roll the dough into balls and place them on the prepared baking sheets 3 inches apart.

Step 6

Bake one batch at a time. Transfer to the oven and bake for 8 minutes. The cookies will still be very soft. Remove from the oven and top each cookie with some of the remaining marshmallows and chocolate chips.

Step 7

Return to the oven and bake for 7 to 10 minutes more, or until the cookies are golden on the edges and soft in the middle.

Step 8

Let the cookies cool on the baking sheet for 10 minutes, then gently transfer them to a wire rack to cool completely.

Step 9

Keep the cookies in an airtight container at room temperature for up to 5 days or freeze for up to 1 month.

The Softest Peanut Butter Cookies

MAKES 24 COOKIES

Prep time: 1 hour 15 minutes
 Cook time: 12 minutes per batch

Ingredients:

- 156 grams All-Purpose Flour Blend

- ½ teaspoon baking soda
- ½ teaspoon xanthan gum
- 8 tablespoons (1 stick) butter or nondairy alternative
- 100 grams light brown sugar
- 50 grams cane sugar or granulated sugar, plus 2 tablespoons
- 180 grams creamy gluten-free peanut butter
- 1 large egg

- 1 teaspoon vanilla extract

Directions:

Step 1

In a small bowl, whisk the flour, baking soda, and xanthan gum to combine.

Step 2

In a large bowl, using a handheld electric mixer on medium speed, cream together the butter, brown sugar, and 50 grams of cane sugar. Add the peanut butter and mix until smooth and creamy. Add the egg and vanilla. Mix until combined.

Step 3

Slowly add the flour mixture and mix until combined. Do not overmix. Cover the bowl with plastic wrap and refrigerate for at least 1 hour.

Step 4

Preheat the oven to 350°F. Line 2 baking sheets with parchment paper or silicone baking mats.

Step 5

Place the remaining 2 tablespoons of cane sugar in a small bowl.

Step 6

Using a 1-inch ice cream scoop, scoop the cookies and gently roll them in the cane sugar to coat lightly. Place the cookies on the prepared baking sheets 3 inches apart. Using the tines of a fork, make a crisscross imprint on each one.

Step 7

Baking one batch at a time, bake for 10 to 12 minutes, or until the edges are slightly browned. The cookies will still be very soft and may have small cracks.

Step 8

Let the cookies cool on the baking sheet to continue baking without becoming overdone. Gently transfer to a wire rack. Keep in an airtight container at room temperature for up to 7 days.

Dunkable Chocolate Chip Cookies

MAKES 34 COOKIES

Prep time: 45 minutes

Cook time: 12 minutes per batch

Ingredients:

- 210 grams All-Purpose Flour Blend

- 1 teaspoon baking soda
- ½ teaspoon xanthan gum

- ½ teaspoon salt
- 51 grams shortening
- 133 grams light brown sugar
- 1 large egg
- 2 tablespoons maple syrup
- 2 teaspoons vanilla extract
- ½ teaspoon apple cider vinegar
- 225 grams semisweet chocolate chips or nondairy alternative

Directions:

Step 1

Line 2 baking sheets with parchment paper or silicone baking mats.

Step 2

In a small bowl, whisk the flour, baking soda, xanthan gum, and salt to combine.

Step 3

In a medium bowl, using a handheld electric mixer on medium speed, cream together the shortening and brown sugar. Add the egg, maple syrup, vanilla, and apple cider vinegar. Mix again until combined. Add the flour mixture and mix to form a dough. Using a spatula, fold in the chocolate chips.

Step 4

Using a 1-inch ice cream scoop, scoop the cookies onto one of the prepared baking sheets. It's okay if they are close together. Refrigerate for 30 minutes.

Step 5

Preheat the oven to 375°F.

Step 6

Transfer half of the chilled cookies onto the second prepared baking sheet, placing them 3 inches apart. Leave the remaining cookies in the refrigerator.

Step 7

Bake the first batch for 10 to 12 minutes, or until lightly browned on the sides.

Step 8

Let the cookies cool on the baking sheet for 10 minutes, then transfer to a wire rack to cool completely.

Step 9

Refill the baking sheet with the chilled cookies from the fridge and bake as directed.

Thin Mint Copycat Cookies

MAKES 28 COOKIES

Prep time: 15 minutes, plus 30 minutes to chill

Cook time: 10 minutes per batch

Ingredients:

FOR THE COOKIES

- 190 grams All-Purpose Flour Blend
- 75 grams Dutch-process cocoa powder
- 1 teaspoon baking powder
- ½ teaspoon xanthan gum
- ¼ teaspoon salt
- 179 grams shortening
- 200 grams cane sugar or granulated sugar
- 1 large egg
- 1 teaspoon vanilla extract
- ¼ teaspoon peppermint extract

FOR THE COATING

- 360 grams semisweet chocolate chips or nondairy alternative
- ½ teaspoon coconut oil, melted
- ¼ teaspoon peppermint extract

Directions:

TO MAKE THE COOKIES

Step 1

Preheat the oven to 350°F. Line 2 baking sheets with parchment paper. Cut two additional large sheets of parchment for rolling the dough.

Step 2

In a medium bowl, whisk the flour, cocoa powder, baking powder, xanthan gum, and salt to combine.

Step 3

In a large bowl, using a handheld electric mixer on medium speed, cream together the shortening and sugar, stopping to scrape down the bowl as needed. Add the egg, vanilla, and peppermint extract and mix until combined. Add the flour mixture and mix until combined. The dough will look slightly sticky.

Step 4

Transfer the dough to one sheet of parchment paper and place the other on top. Roll the dough to a large round about ¼ inch thick. Using a 2-inch round cookie cutter, cut out the cookies and place them on the baking sheets. Reroll the remaining dough and repeat until no dough is left.

Step 5

Baking one sheet at a time, bake for 8 to 10 minutes.

Step 6

Let the cookies cool on the pan for 10 minutes, then transfer to a wire rack. They will be soft at first but will crisp as they cool.

TO MAKE THE COATING

Step 7

In a medium saucepan, melt the chocolate over medium-low heat, stirring constantly so it does not burn. Stir in the coconut oil and peppermint extract.

Step 8

Dip each cookie in the melted chocolate and coat completely. Using a fork, lift them out of the chocolate, letting any excess fall back into the pan. Place the dipped cookies back on the parchment-lined baking sheets. Refrigerate for 30 minutes to help the chocolate set.

Step 9

Just like traditional Thin Mints, these cookies are best eaten cold. Refrigerate leftovers in an airtight container for up to 1 week or freeze for up to 1 month.

Blackberry Shortbread Thumbprints

MAKES 24 COOKIES
Prep time: 20 minutes, plus 30 minutes to chill
 Cook time: 14 minutes per batch

Ingredients:

- 250 grams All-Purpose Flour Blend

- 1 teaspoon xanthan gum
- ½ teaspoon baking powder
- 136 grams shortening
- 133 grams cane sugar or granulated sugar
- 1 teaspoon vanilla extract
- ½ teaspoon orange extract
- ½ cup blackberry jam

- Glaze (from Cinnamon Roll Pancakes)

Directions:

Step 1

Line 2 baking sheets with parchment paper or silicone baking mats.

Step 2

In a small bowl, whisk the flour, xanthan gum, and baking powder to combine.

Step 3

In a large bowl, using a handheld electric mixer on medium speed, cream together the shortening and sugar. Add the vanilla and orange extract and mix to combine. Add flour mixture and mix to form a dough.

Step 4

Using 1-tablespoon portions, roll the dough into balls and place them on the prepared baking sheets. Gently make a thumbprint in the center of each cookie. Smooth any cracks along the outer edges with your fingers. Fill each thumbprint with about ½ teaspoon of jam. Refrigerate for 30 minutes.

Step 5

Preheat the oven to 350°F.

Step 6

Baking one batch at a time, bake for 12 to 14 minutes, or until the edges are slightly browned.

Step 7

Let the cookies cool on the pan for 5 to 10 minutes, then gently transfer to a wire rack to cool completely.

Step 8

Using a fork, drizzle the glaze over the cookies. Let set and dry for about 1 hour. Keep in an airtight container at room temperature for up to 5 days, or freeze for up to 1 month.

Easy Frosted Sugar Cookies

MAKES 16 COOKIES
Prep time: 1 hour 20 minutes
 Cook time: 13 minutes per batch

Ingredients:

FOR THE COOKIES

312 grams All-Purpose Flour Blend , plus more for dusting

½ teaspoon xanthan gum

½ teaspoon baking powder

¼ teaspoon salt

102 grams shortening

150 grams cane sugar or granulated sugar

1 large egg

2 teaspoons vanilla extract

¼ teaspoon orange extract

¼ cup plus 1 tablespoon cold water

FOR THE FROSTING

240 grams powdered sugar

¼ cup whole milk or coconut milk beverage

½ teaspoon vanilla extract

Directions:

TO MAKE THE COOKIES

Step 1

In a small bowl, whisk the flour, xanthan gum, baking powder, and salt to combine.

Step 2

In a large bowl, using a handheld electric mixer on medium speed, cream together the shortening and sugar. Add the egg, vanilla, and orange extract and mix to combine. Slowly add the flour mixture and cold water. Stir until coarse crumbs form. Continue to form the dough by hand. The warmth of your hands will help the dough come together.

Step 3

Divide the dough into 4 equal portions, wrap each in plastic wrap, and chill for 30 minutes to 1 hour. Any longer and your dough will be too hard to work with and you will need to let it sit on the counter for 5 to 10 minutes so it is easier to work with.

Step 4

Preheat the oven to 350°F. Line 2 baking sheets with parchment paper or silicone baking mats.

Step 5

Place two sheets of parchment paper on a work surface and dust them with flour. Place one dough portion between the two sheets of parchment and roll it to ¼-inch thickness. Using cookie cutters, cut the dough into desired shapes and transfer them to the prepared baking sheets. Gather the scraps and repeat the steps with the remaining 3 dough portions.

Step 6

Bake for 11 to 13 minutes. The cookies will be soft but very lightly browned around the edges.

Step 7

Let the cookies cool on the baking sheet for 10 minutes, then use a spatula to gently transfer them to a wire rack to cool completely.

TO MAKE THE FROSTING

Step 8

In a medium bowl, stir together the powdered sugar, milk, and vanilla until smooth.

Step 9

Dip each cookie top into the icing, then transfer to a wire rack. Allow the icing to set for about 1 hour.

Step 10

Keep the cookies in an airtight container at room temperature for up to 4 days. They can be frozen without icing for up to 1 month in a freezer bag. Separating the cookies with parchment paper before freezing helps keep them fresh.

Cranberry Oatmeal Cookies

MAKES 24 COOKIES

Prep time: 15 minutes

 Cook time: 10 minutes per batch

Ingredients:

- 300 grams certified gluten-free rolled oats

- 156 grams All-Purpose Flour Blend

- 1 teaspoon baking soda
- 1 teaspoon ground cinnamon
- ¼ teaspoon ground nutmeg
- ¼ teaspoon xanthan gum
- ¼ teaspoon salt
- 16 tablespoons (2 sticks) butter or nondairy alternative
- 200 grams light brown sugar
- 2 large eggs
- 1 teaspoon vanilla extract
- 150 grams dried cranberries

Directions:

Step 1

Preheat the oven to 350°F. Line 2 baking sheets with parchment paper or silicone baking mats.

Step 2

In a food processor, pulse the oats 5 or 6 times to break them down.

Step 3

In a medium bowl, whisk the flour, baking soda, cinnamon, nutmeg, xanthan gum, and salt to combine. Whisk in the oats and set aside.

Step 4

In a large bowl, using a handheld electric mixer on medium speed, cream together the butter and brown sugar. Add the eggs and vanilla. Mix well to combine. Beat in the flour mixture in two additions and mix to form the dough. Using a spatula, fold in the cranberries.

Step 5

Using tablespoon-size portions, roll the dough into balls and place them on the prepared baking sheets 3 inches apart.

Step 6

Baking one batch at a time, bake for 10 minutes, or until the edges are crispy.

Step 7

Let cookies cool on the baking sheets for 10 minutes, then gently transfer them to a wire rack to cool completely. Keep in an airtight container at room temperature for up to 5 days.

Sensational Snickerdoodles

MAKES 24 COOKIES

Prep time: 1 hour 15 minutes
 Cook time: 13 minutes per batch

Ingredients:

- 190 grams All-Purpose Flour Blend
- 1 teaspoon xanthan gum
- 1 teaspoon cream of tartar
- 2 teaspoons ground cinnamon, divided
- ½ teaspoon baking soda
- ½ teaspoon salt
- 8 tablespoons (1 stick) butter or nondairy alternative
- 2 ounces cream cheese or nondairy alternative
- 150 grams cane sugar or granulated sugar, plus 2 tablespoons
- 1 large egg
- 2 teaspoons vanilla extract

Directions:

Step 1

In a small bowl, whisk the flour, xanthan gum, cream of tartar, 1 teaspoon of cinnamon, the baking soda, and salt to combine.

Step 2

In a large bowl, using a handheld electric mixer on medium speed, cream together the butter and cream cheese until smooth. Mix in 150 grams of sugar until well combined. Add the egg and vanilla and mix to combine, stopping to scrape down the bowl as needed.

Step 3

Beat the flour mixture into the cream cheese mixture in two additions, mixing to form a dough. This dough will be thick and pasty. Transfer the dough to an airtight container and refrigerate for at least 1 hour, or overnight for best results.

Step 4

Preheat the oven to 350°F. Line 2 baking sheets with parchment paper. (I recommend parchment because these cookies are so soft that the silicone mats will grip the edges but leave a hollow middle.)

Step 5

In a small bowl, stir together the remaining 1 teaspoon of cinnamon and the remaining 2 tablespoons of sugar.

Step 6

Using tablespoon-size portions, roll the chilled dough into balls. Roll the balls in the cinnamon sugar and place them on the prepared baking sheet 3 inches apart. Fill both baking sheets. While one sheet is in the oven, place the other in the refrigerator.

Step 7

Bake for 11 to 13 minutes, or until the edges are set. The cookies will still be soft. Do not overbake.

Step 8

Let the cookies cool completely on the baking sheet, where they will continue baking without becoming overdone. Bake the second batch as directed. Keep in an airtight container at room temperature for up to 5 days.

Biscotti

MAKES 16 BISCOTTI

Prep time: 15 minutes

Cook time: 45 minutes

Ingredients:

- 190 grams All-Purpose Flour Blend

- 60 grams brown rice flour
- 1 teaspoon baking powder
- ½ teaspoon xanthan gum
- ½ teaspoon salt
- 4 tablespoons butter or nondairy alternative
- 150 grams cane sugar or granulated sugar
- 3 large eggs, divided
- 1½ teaspoons vanilla extract
- ½ teaspoon orange extract

Directions:

Step 1

Preheat the oven to 350°F. Line 2 baking sheets with parchment paper or silicone baking mats.

Step 2

In a medium bowl, whisk the all-purpose flour, brown rice flour, baking powder, xanthan gum, and salt to combine.

Step 3

In a large bowl, using a handheld electric mixer on medium speed, cream together the butter and sugar. Add 2 of the eggs and the vanilla and orange extracts, and mix until combined. Add the flour mixture and mix until combined, stopping to scrape down the bowl as needed. Your dough will resemble a very thick batter.

Step 4

Add about 1 tablespoon of water to a piping bag and rub the bag from the outside to spread the water inside the bag. This will help the dough slide through the bag. Fill the piping bag with the biscotti dough. Cut the tip of the bag a little bit bigger than 1 inch wide. Squeeze the dough into two equal-size logs onto one baking sheet. With wet fingertips, flatten the logs until they are about 1 inch in height.

Step 5

In a small bowl, whisk the remaining egg and 1 tablespoon water to create an egg wash. Using a pastry brush, lightly brush the egg wash over the top of each log.

Step 6

Bake for 20 to 25 minutes. Remove from the oven, but leave the oven on.

Step 7

Let the logs cool on the baking sheet for at least 30 minutes.

Step 8

With a sharp nonserrated knife, cut each log on the diagonal into ¾-inch-thick slices. Push down on the knife rather than saw, to prevent the cookies from breaking. Place each cookie on the second prepared baking sheet, cut-side up.

Step 9

Return to the oven and bake for 12 to 14 minutes, or until golden, with crisp edges.

Step 10

Let the biscotti cool on the pan for about 10 minutes, then transfer to a wire rack to cool completely. They will continue to crisp as they cool. Keep in an airtight container at room temperature for 1 to 2 weeks or freeze for up to 3 months.

Decadent Chocolate Cobbler

MAKES 1 (9-BY-9-INCH) COBBLER

Prep time: 15 minutes

Cook time: 30 minutes

Ingredients:

FOR THE COBBLER

- Shortening, for preparing the pan

- 125 grams All-Purpose Flour Blend

- 1 tablespoon arrowroot
- 2 teaspoons baking powder
- 1½ tablespoons Dutch-process cocoa powder
- ½ teaspoon salt
- ¼ teaspoon xanthan gum
- 133 grams cane sugar or granulated sugar
- ½ cup whole milk or coconut milk beverage
- 2 tablespoons butter or nondairy alternative, melted
- 1 teaspoon vanilla extract

FOR THE TOPPING

- 50 grams cane sugar or granulated sugar
- 100 grams light brown sugar
- 1 tablespoon Dutch-process cocoa powder
- ¼ teaspoon salt
- 1 cup boiling water

Directions:

TO MAKE THE COBBLER

Step 1

Preheat the oven to 350°F. Grease a 9-by-9-inch baking pan with shortening.

Step 2

In a medium bowl, whisk the flour, arrowroot, baking powder, cocoa powder, salt, xanthan gum, and sugar to combine. Using a spatula, stir in the milk, melted butter, and vanilla, mixing just until combined.

Step 3

Spread the mixture into the prepared pan.

TO MAKE THE TOPPING

Step 4

In a small bowl, whisk the cane sugar, brown sugar, cocoa powder, and salt to combine. Sprinkle the topping over the batter. Do not stir.

Step 5

Pour the boiling water evenly on top of the batter and topping. Do not stir.

Step 6

Bake for 30 minutes, or until the top is almost set. The cake should rise to the top and a creamy layer will form at the bottom. Serve warm.

Step 7

Keep leftovers covered and refrigerated for up to 3 days. Reheat to serve.

Pear Pecan Crisp

MAKES 1 (9-BY-9-INCH) CRISP

Prep time: 15 minutes
 Cook time: 25 minutes

Ingredients:

- Shortening, for preparing the pan

FOR THE FILLING

- 32 grams All-Purpose Flour Blend

- 2 tablespoons light brown sugar
- 1 teaspoon vanilla extract
- 1 teaspoon ground cinnamon
- ¼ teaspoon xanthan gum
- ¼ teaspoon salt
- 6 firm-ripe pears, peeled and cut into thin, bite-size pieces
- 1 tablespoon fresh lemon juice

FOR THE TOPPING

- 32 grams All-Purpose Flour Blend

- 100 grams light brown sugar
- 50 grams certified gluten-free rolled oats
- 32 grams chopped pecans
- ¼ teaspoon xanthan gum
- 5 tablespoons plus 1 teaspoon butter or nondairy alternative, melted

Directions:

Step 1

Preheat the oven to 375°F. Grease a 9-by-9-inch pan with shortening.

TO MAKE THE FILLING

Step 2

In a small bowl, whisk the flour, brown sugar, vanilla, cinnamon, xanthan gum, and salt to combine.

Step 3

In a medium bowl, combine the pears and lemon juice. Add the flour mixture and, using a spatula, gently fold until the pear pieces are coated.

Step 4

Spread the filling in the prepared pan.

TO MAKE THE TOPPING

Step 5

In a medium bowl, whisk the flour, brown sugar, oats, pecans, and xanthan gum to combine. Using a spoon or spatula, stir in the melted butter. Evenly sprinkle the topping over the pears.

Step 6

Bake for 20 to 25 minutes, until the pears are tender and the crust is golden.

Step 7

Serve warm. Refrigerate leftovers, covered, for up to 3 days. Reheat to serve.

Toasted Coconut Apple Raspberry Crisp

MAKES 1 (9-BY-9-INCH) CRISP
Prep time: 20 minutes
 Cook time: 37 minutes

Ingredients:

FOR THE TOASTED COCONUT

- 50 grams shredded coconut

FOR THE FILLING

- Shortening, for preparing the pan
- 2 Granny Smith or Honeycrisp apples, peeled and very thinly sliced
- 62 grams raspberries
- 1 tablespoon fresh lemon juice
- 1 teaspoon ground cinnamon

FOR THE OAT TOPPING

- 50 grams certified gluten-free rolled oats

- 2 tablespoons All-Purpose Flour Blend

- 2 tablespoons light brown sugar
- ¼ teaspoon xanthan gum
- 1 tablespoon maple syrup
- 2 tablespoons butter or nondairy alternative

Directions:

TO TOAST THE COCONUT

Step 1

Preheat the oven to 325°F. Line a baking sheet with parchment paper.

Step 2

Spread the coconut into a thin layer on the parchment and toast for 5 to 7 minutes until golden. Set aside.

Step 3

Leave the oven on and increase the temperature to 350°F.

TO MAKE THE FILLING

Step 4

Grease a 9-by-9-inch pan with shortening.

Step 5

In a medium bowl, combine the apples, raspberries, lemon juice, and cinnamon. Using a spatula, fold together the fruit and spread it in the prepared pan.

TO MAKE THE OAT TOPPING

Step 6

In a small bowl, whisk the oats, flour, brown sugar, and xanthan gum to combine. Add the maple syrup and butter. Using a pastry cutter, cut the butter into the mixture until crumbs form.

Step 7

Sprinkle the topping evenly over the fruit.

Step 8

Bake for 25 to 30 minutes, or until the topping is golden brown.

Step 9

Let the crisp cool for about 10 minutes. Sprinkle the toasted coconut over the top and serve. Refrigerate leftovers, covered, for up to 3 days.

Strawberry Streusel Crisp

MAKES 1 (11-BY-7-INCH) CRISP

Prep time: 15 minutes

Cook time: 45 minutes

Ingredients:

Shortening, for preparing the pan

FOR THE FILLING

- 100 grams cane sugar or granulated sugar
- 32 grams All-Purpose Flour Blend
- ¼ teaspoon xanthan gum
- ¼ teaspoon salt
- 800 grams sliced strawberries
- 1 tablespoon vanilla extract

FOR THE STREUSEL TOPPING

- 133 grams light brown sugar
- 85 grams All-Purpose Flour Blend
- 1 teaspoon ground cinnamon
- ¼ teaspoon xanthan gum
- ¼ teaspoon salt
- 8 tablespoons (1 stick) cold butter or nondairy alternative
- 66 grams gluten-free certified oats

Directions:

Step 1

Preheat the oven to 350°F. Grease an 11-by-7-inch pan with shortening.

TO MAKE THE FILLING

Step 2

In a large bowl, whisk the cane sugar, flour, xanthan gum, and salt to combine. Add the strawberries and vanilla. Using a spatula, gently toss everything together.

Step 3

Pour the strawberry mixture into the prepared baking dish and refrigerate until needed.

TO MAKE THE STREUSEL TOPPING

Step 4

In a medium bowl, whisk the brown sugar, flour, cinnamon, xanthan gum, and salt to combine. Smooth any clumps of brown sugar.

Step 5

Cut the butter into pieces and add it to the flour mixture. Using a pastry cutter, cut the butter into the flour mixture until crumbs form. Using a spatula, fold in the oats.

Step 6

Remove the filling from the refrigerator and cover it evenly with the topping.

Step 7

Bake for 40 to 45 minutes, or until the topping is crisp and the filling is bubbling.

Step 8

Let the streusel crisp cool on a wire rack for about 10 minutes. Serve warm or cooled. Refrigerate leftovers, covered, for up to 3 days.

Skillet Cherry Cobbler

MAKES 1 (12-INCH) COBBLER

Prep time: 20 minutes

 Cook time: 45 minutes

Ingredients:

FOR THE SIMPLE SYRUP

- 100 grams cane sugar or granulated sugar

FOR THE FILLING

- 100 grams cane sugar or granulated sugar

- 32 grams All-Purpose Flour Blend

- ¼ teaspoon xanthan gum
- ¼ teaspoon ground cinnamon
- ¼ teaspoon ground nutmeg
- ¼ teaspoon salt
- 1,350 grams frozen cherries
- 1 teaspoon vanilla extract

FOR THE TOPPING

- 190 grams All-Purpose Flour Blend

- 100 grams cane sugar or granulated sugar
- 1½ teaspoons baking powder
- ½ teaspoon xanthan gum

- ¼ teaspoon baking soda
- ¼ teaspoon salt
- ¾ cup whole milk or coconut milk beverage
- 4 tablespoons butter or nondairy alternative, melted
- ½ teaspoon apple cider vinegar
- 2 tablespoons raw turbinado sugar

Directions:

Step 1

Preheat the oven to 425°F.

TO MAKE THE SIMPLE SYRUP

Step 2

In a small saucepan, stir together the cane sugar and ½ cup water. Cook over medium-high heat, stirring until the sugar dissolves, then bring to a boil. Boil for 5 minutes. Transfer to a heatproof bowl to cool.

TO MAKE THE FILLING

Step 3

In a large bowl, whisk the cane sugar, flour, xanthan gum, cinnamon, nutmeg, and salt to combine. Add the frozen cherries and stir to coat. Add the simple syrup and vanilla. Mix to combine.

TO MAKE THE TOPPING

Step 4

In a medium bowl, whisk the flour, cane sugar, baking powder, xanthan gum, baking soda, and salt to combine. Using a spatula, mix in the milk, melted butter, and vinegar until just combined.

Step 5

Pour the sugar-coated cherries into a 12-inch cast-iron skillet and spread them evenly.

Step 6

Using a 1-inch ice cream scoop, drop portions of the topping onto the filling, spacing them about ½ inch apart. Using a spatula, spread the topping over the entire skillet, covering the cherries. Sprinkle the top with the turbinado sugar.

Step 7

Bake for 30 to 35 minutes, or until the topping is golden brown and the filling is thick and glossy.

Step 8

Let the cobbler cool for about 10 minutes before serving warm. Refrigerate leftovers in an airtight container for up to 3 days.

Very Berry Cobbler

MAKES 1 (9-BY-13-INCH) COBBLER

Prep time: 20 minutes

Cook time: 55 minutes

Ingredients:

Shortening, for preparing the pan

FOR THE FILLING

- 2 tablespoons All-Purpose Flour Blend
- ¼ teaspoon xanthan gum
- 50 grams cane sugar or granulated sugar
- 2 teaspoons fresh lemon juice
- 2 teaspoons vanilla extract
- 200 grams blueberries
- 230 grams blackberries
- 250 grams raspberries

FOR THE TOPPING

- 156 grams All-Purpose Flour Blend , plus more for dusting
- ½ teaspoon xanthan gum
- 1 teaspoon baking powder
- ¼ teaspoon salt
- 50 grams cane sugar or granulated sugar
- 67 grams shortening
- 1 large egg yolk
- ¼ cup buttermilk, plus 2 tablespoons, or ¼ cup plus 2 tablespoons coconut milk beverage plus 2 teaspoons apple cider vinegar (see here)
- Raw turbinado sugar, for sprinkling

Directions:

Step 1

Preheat the oven to 350°F. Grease a 9-by-13-inch pan with shortening.

TO MAKE THE FILLING

Step 2

In a small bowl, whisk the flour and xanthan gum to combine. Add the sugar, lemon juice, and vanilla and mix well. If it's clumpy, don't worry.

Step 3

In a large bowl, combine the blueberries, blackberries, and raspberries. Pour the flour mixture on top and use a spatula to gently fold into the berries. Transfer the mixed berries to the prepared pan, cover with aluminum foil, and refrigerate until needed.

TO MAKE THE TOPPING

Step 4

Place two sheets of parchment paper on a work surface and dust them with flour.

Step 5

In a medium bowl, whisk the flour and xanthan gum to combine. Add the baking powder, salt, and sugar. Whisk well.

Step 6

Using a pastry cutter, cut the shortening into the flour mixture until it forms coarse crumbs. Add the egg yolk and ¼ cup of buttermilk. Form the dough by hand. Transfer it to the flour-dusted work surface. Pat the dough into a flat rectangle, dusting the top with a little bit of flour. Place the second sheet of parchment over the top. Using a rolling pin, flatten the dough to about the size of your baking pan.

Step 7

Remove the berries from the refrigerator. Lift the top layer of parchment, place your right hand underneath the bottom layer of parchment paper and your left hand on top of the dough, and gently flip the dough over and on top of the berries. Peel off the remaining piece of parchment and adjust the edges of the dough to fit nicely over the berries in your pan.

Step 8

Using a pastry brush, brush the dough with the remaining 2 tablespoons of buttermilk. Sprinkle with turbinado sugar.

Step 9

Bake for 45 to 55 minutes, or until the top is golden.

Step 10

Let the cobbler cool on a wire rack for 10 minutes before serving. Refrigerate leftovers, covered, for up to 5 days.

Peach Cobbler

MAKES 1 (11-BY-7-INCH) COBBLER

Prep time: 20 minutes

Cook time: 40 minutes

Ingredients:

- Shortening, for preparing the pan

FOR THE FILLING

- 1,000 grams sliced peeled peaches (about 10 peaches)
- 50 grams light brown sugar

- 2 tablespoons All-Purpose Flour Blend

- ¼ teaspoon xanthan gum

FOR THE TOPPING

- 250 grams All-Purpose Flour Blend

- 1 tablespoon baking powder
- 1 teaspoon xanthan gum
- 1 teaspoon ground cinnamon
- ¼ teaspoon salt
- ½ cup whole milk or coconut milk beverage
- 1 large egg
- 1 teaspoon apple cider vinegar
- 8 tablespoons (1 stick) cold butter or nondairy alternative
- 2 tablespoons raw turbinado sugar

Directions:

Step 1

Preheat the oven to 425°F. Grease an 11-by-7-inch baking dish or a 9-by-9-inch pan with shortening.

TO MAKE THE FILLING

Step 2

Place the peaches in a large bowl and pour the brown sugar over them.

Step 3

In a small bowl, whisk the flour and xanthan gum to combine and add it to the peaches. Stir to combine everything.

TO MAKE THE TOPPING

Step 4

In a medium bowl, whisk the flour, baking powder, xanthan gum, cinnamon, and salt to combine.

Step 5

In a small bowl, whisk the milk, egg, and vinegar.

Step 6

Using a pastry cutter, cut the cold butter into pieces and mix it into the flour mixture. Drizzle in the egg mixture and, using a spatula, stir just until combined. It should be lumpy.

Step 7

Pour the peaches into the prepared baking dish.

Step 8

Using a 1-inch ice cream scoop, drop chunks of the topping over the peaches, spacing them about ½ inch apart. Using a spatula, spread the topping over the entire pan. Sprinkle the turbinado sugar evenly over the top. Loosely cover the pan with aluminum foil.

Step 9

Bake for 30 minutes. Remove the foil and bake for 10 minutes more until golden.

Step 10

Serve warm or at room temperature. Refrigerate leftovers, covered, for up to 3 days.

Vanilla Cupcakes

MAKES 12 CUPCAKES

Prep time: 15 minutes

Cook time: 20 minutes

Ingredients:

FOR THE CUPCAKES

- 190 grams All-Purpose Flour Blend
- 1 teaspoon baking powder
- ½ teaspoon xanthan gum
- ¼ teaspoon baking soda
- ¼ teaspoon salt
- 3 large egg whites
- 200 grams cane sugar or granulated sugar
- ½ cup avocado oil or canola oil
- ¼ cup whole milk or coconut milk beverage
- 1 tablespoon vanilla extract

FOR THE FROSTING

- 134 grams shortening
- 1 teaspoon vanilla extract
- 480 grams powdered sugar, plus more as needed

Directions:

TO MAKE THE CUPCAKES

Step 1

Preheat the oven to 350°F. Line a 12-cup muffin tin with cupcake liners.

Step 2

In a small bowl, whisk the flour, baking powder, xanthan gum, baking soda, and salt to combine.

Step 3

In a large bowl, using a handheld electric mixer, whip the egg whites until they form a soft peak. Add the cane sugar, oil, milk, and vanilla. Mix well. Add the flour mixture and mix until combined.

Step 4

Evenly divide the batter between the prepared muffin cups, filling them three-quarters full.

Step 5

Bake for 18 to 20 minutes, or until a toothpick inserted into the center of a cupcake comes out clean.

Step 6

Let the cupcakes cool in the pan for 10 minutes, then transfer them to a wire rack to cool completely.

TO MAKE THE FROSTING

Step 7

While the cupcakes are cooling, in a large bowl, using a handheld electric mixer on medium speed, cream together the shortening and vanilla until smooth.

Step 8

Add the powdered sugar and mix on low speed until smooth and creamy, adding 1 tablespoon of water at a time until you get the desired consistency. If the frosting is too thick, add 1 tablespoon more of water; if it is too thin, add 1 tablespoon of powdered sugar.

Step 9

Fill a piping bag fitted your desired tip with the frosting and decorate each cupcake as desired. Keep covered at room temperature for up to 4 days.

Pumpkin Pie Cupcakes

MAKES 12 CUPCAKES

Prep time: 15 minutes

Cook time: 30 minutes

Ingredients:

FOR THE CUPCAKES

- 125 grams All-Purpose Flour Blend

- 2 teaspoons pumpkin pie spice
- 1 teaspoon ground cinnamon
- ½ teaspoon xanthan gum
- ¼ teaspoon ground cloves
- ¼ teaspoon baking powder
- ¼ teaspoon baking soda

- ¼ teaspoon salt
- 1 (7.4-ounce) can sweetened condensed coconut milk
- 150 grams cane sugar or granulated sugar
- 2 large eggs
- 1 (15-ounce) can pumpkin puree

FOR THE COCONUT WHIPPED CREAM

- 1 (14-ounce) can coconut cream, chilled overnight
- 2 tablespoons powdered sugar

Directions:

TO MAKE THE CUPCAKES

Step 1

Preheat the oven to 350°F. Line a 12-cup muffin tin with cupcake liners.

Step 2

In a small bowl, whisk the flour, pumpkin pie spice, cinnamon, xanthan gum, cloves, baking powder, baking soda, and salt to combine.

Step 3

In a large bowl, using a spatula, mix the condensed coconut milk and cane sugar. Stir all the clumps out of the milk. Add the eggs and mix well. Add the pumpkin puree and the flour mixture. Stir just until combined. Do not overmix.

Step 4

Scoop the batter evenly into the prepared muffin cups.

Step 5

Bake for 28 to 30 minutes, or until a toothpick inserted into the center of a cupcake comes out clean.

Step 6

Let the cupcakes cool in the pan for 30 minutes.

Gingerbread Cupcakes

MAKES 12 CUPCAKES

Prep time: 25 minutes

Cook time: 22 minutes

Ingredients:

FOR THE CUPCAKES

- 167 grams All-Purpose Flour Blend

- 2 tablespoons arrowroot
- 1½ teaspoons ground cinnamon
- ½ teaspoon xanthan gum
- ½ teaspoon baking powder
- ½ teaspoon baking soda
- ½ teaspoon ground ginger
- ½ teaspoon ground nutmeg
- ½ teaspoon ground cloves
- ¼ teaspoon salt
- ½ cup avocado oil or canola oil
- 100 grams light brown sugar
- ½ cup whole milk or coconut milk beverage
- ½ cup maple syrup
- 1 large egg
- 1 teaspoon vanilla extract
- ½ teaspoon apple cider vinegar

FOR THE CREAM CHEESE FROSTING

- 102 grams shortening
- 4 ounces cream cheese or nondairy alternative
- 480 grams powdered sugar
- 1 teaspoon vanilla extract
- 4 tablespoons whole milk or coconut milk beverage

Directions:

TO MAKE THE CUPCAKES

Step 1

Preheat the oven to 350°F. Line a 12-cup muffin tin with cupcake liners.

Step 2

In a medium bowl, whisk the flour, arrowroot, cinnamon, xanthan gum, baking powder, baking soda, ginger, nutmeg, cloves, and salt to combine.

Step 3

In a large bowl, using a handheld electric mixer, beat the oil and brown sugar to blend. Add the milk, maple syrup, egg, vanilla, and vinegar. Mix well. Beat in the flour mixture in two additions, mixing to combine, and stopping to scrape down the bowl as needed, making sure there are no brown sugar clumps.

Step 4

Evenly divide the batter between the prepared muffin cups, filling them two-thirds full.

Step 5

Bake for 20 to 22 minutes, or until a toothpick inserted into the center of a cupcake comes out clean.

Step 6

Let the cupcakes cool in the pan for at least 10 minutes, then transfer to a wire rack to cool completely.

TO MAKE THE CREAM CHEESE FROSTING

Step 7

In a large bowl, using a handheld electric mixer on medium speed, cream together the shortening and cream cheese. Add the powdered sugar and vanilla. Mix as you add the milk by the tablespoon until smooth and creamy.

Step 8

Frost the cupcakes. Refrigerate leftovers, covered, for up to 5 days.

Thin Mint Cupcakes

MAKES 12 CUPCAKES

Prep time: 1 hour

Cook time: about 20 minutes

Ingredients:

FOR THE CUPCAKES

- 95 grams All-Purpose Flour Blend

- 50 grams Dutch-process cocoa powder
- 1 tablespoon arrowroot
- ¾ teaspoon baking powder
- ½ teaspoon baking soda
- ½ teaspoon xanthan gum
- ¼ teaspoon salt
- 150 grams cane sugar or granulated sugar
- 50 grams light brown sugar
- 2 large eggs
- ⅓ cup avocado oil or canola oil
- ½ cup whole milk or coconut milk beverage
- 2 teaspoons vanilla extract
- ½ teaspoon apple cider vinegar
- ½ recipe Thin Mint Copycat Cookies , prepared through step 4 and rolled into 12 balls

FOR THE MINT FROSTING

- 136 grams shortening

- ¼ teaspoon peppermint extract
- 2 drops green food coloring
- 480 grams powdered sugar
- 4 tablespoons whole milk or coconut milk beverage

Directions:

TO MAKE THE CUPCAKES

Step 1

Preheat the oven to 350°F. Line a 12-cup muffin tin with cupcake liners.

Step 2

In a medium bowl, whisk the flour, cocoa powder, arrowroot, baking powder, baking soda, xanthan gum, and salt to combine.

Step 3

In a large bowl, using a whisk or handheld electric mixer, mix the cane sugar, brown sugar, eggs, oil, milk, vanilla, and vinegar. Beat in the flour mixture in two additions, mixing on low speed to blend and stopping to scrape down the bowl as needed, and making sure there are no brown sugar clumps. The batter should be thick.

Step 4

Place 1 cookie dough ball into each prepared muffin cup. Evenly divide the batter over each, filling each cup no more than two-thirds full.

Step 5

Bake for 18 to 20 minutes, or until a toothpick inserted in the side of a cupcake comes out clean. (Be careful to avoid the cookie dough center when testing for doneness.)

Step 6

Let the cupcakes cool in the pan for at least 10 minutes, then transfer to a wire rack to cool completely.

TO MAKE THE MINT FROSTING

Step 7

In a large bowl, using a handheld electric mixer on medium speed, cream the shortening.

Step 8

Add the mint extract, food coloring, and powdered sugar and mix to combine. While mixing, add the milk by the tablespoon and mix until smooth and creamy.

Step 9

Frost the cupcakes. Keep leftovers in an airtight container at room temperature for up to 4 days.

Very Strawberry Cupcakes

MAKES 12 CUPCAKES

Prep time: 1 hour 45 minutes

 Cook time: 42 minutes

Ingredients:

FOR THE STRAWBERRY FILLING

- 250 grams sliced fresh strawberries
- 2 tablespoons cane sugar or granulated sugar

FOR THE CUPCAKES

- 207 grams All-Purpose Flour Blend

- 2 tablespoons arrowroot
- 1 teaspoon xanthan gum
- 1 teaspoon baking soda
- ¼ teaspoon salt
- 8 tablespoons (1 stick) butter or nondairy alternative
- 200 grams cane sugar or granulated sugar
- 3 large egg whites
- 60 grams vanilla Greek yogurt or nondairy alternative
- 2 teaspoons vanilla extract
- ⅓ cup whole milk or coconut milk beverage

FOR THE STRAWBERRY FROSTING

- 34 grams freeze-dried strawberries
- 240 grams powdered sugar
- 68 grams shortening
- 2 to 3 tablespoons whole milk or coconut milk beverage
- 1 teaspoon vanilla extract

Directions:

TO MAKE THE STRAWBERRY FILLING

Step 1

In a small saucepan, combine the strawberries and sugar. Bring to a simmer over medium heat and cook for about 20 minutes, stirring occasionally to prevent burning. The strawberries will reduce and thicken. Transfer to a bowl, cover with plastic wrap, and refrigerate for at least 1 hour.

TO MAKE THE CUPCAKES

Step 2

Preheat the oven to 350°F. Line a 12-cup muffin tin with cupcake liners.

Step 3

In a small bowl, whisk the flour, arrowroot, xanthan gum, baking soda, and salt to combine.

Step 4

In a large bowl, using a handheld electric mixer on medium speed, cream together the butter and cane sugar. Add the egg whites and mix until combined, stopping to scrape down the bowl as needed. Add the yogurt, vanilla, and milk. Mix again.

Step 5

Using a spatula, scrape the sides and the bottom of the bowl to make sure all ingredients at the bottom are mixed in. With the mixer on low speed, slowly add the flour mixture. The batter will look curdled. That's okay.

Step 6

Using a spatula, fold in ½ cup of the strawberry filling (you may have a bit extra leftover) until it is evenly spread through the batter. Evenly divide the batter between the prepared muffin cups, filling each two-thirds full. Do not overfill.

Step 7

Bake for 20 to 22 minutes, or until a toothpick inserted into the center of a cupcake comes out clean.

Step 8

Let the cupcakes cool completely before frosting.

TO MAKE THE STRAWBERRY FROSTING

Step 9

In a food processor, pulse the freeze-dried strawberries to form a fine powder.

Step 10

In a large bowl, using a handheld electric mixer, beat together the powdered sugar, shortening, strawberry powder, milk, and vanilla until smooth.

Step 11

Transfer the frosting to a piping bag with your choice of tip. Frost the cupcakes. Refrigerate leftovers, covered, for up to 5 days.

Fudgy Chocolate Cupcakes

MAKES 12 CUPCAKES

Prep time: 30 minutes

Cook time: 30 minutes

Ingredients:

FOR THE CUPCAKES

- 190 grams All-Purpose Flour Blend

- 25 grams Dutch-process cocoa powder
- 1 teaspoon baking powder
- ½ teaspoon xanthan gum
- ¼ teaspoon salt
- 155 grams dark chocolate chips or nondairy alternative
- 6 tablespoons butter or nondairy alternative
- 200 grams cane sugar or granulated sugar
- 160 grams vanilla Greek yogurt or nondairy alternative
- 2 large eggs
- 2 teaspoons vanilla extract

FOR THE GANACHE

- 270 grams semisweet chocolate chips or nondairy alternative
- ¼ cup coconut oil, melted

Directions:

TO MAKE THE CUPCAKES

Step 1

Preheat the oven to 350°F. Line a 12-cup muffin tin with cupcake liners.

Step 2

In a medium bowl, whisk the flour, cocoa powder, baking powder, xanthan gum, and salt to combine.

Step 3

In a small saucepan, combine the chocolate chips and butter. Melt over low heat, stirring constantly until smooth. Set aside.

Step 4

In a large bowl, using a handheld electric mixer, beat the sugar, yogurt, eggs, and vanilla until well mixed. Add the chocolate mixture and continue beating. Beat in the flour mixture in two additions. Mix until combined. The batter will be very thick.

Step 5

Evenly divide the batter between the prepared muffin cups. With a slightly damp finger, smooth the top of each.

Step 6

Bake for 18 to 20 minutes, or until a toothpick inserted into a cupcake comes out clean.

Step 7

Let the cupcakes cool completely before frosting.

TO MAKE THE GANACHE

Step 8

In a small saucepan, combine the chocolate chips and coconut oil. Melt over low heat, stirring until smooth.

Step 9

Dip the top of each cupcake in the chocolate ganache. Once you have dipped all 12 cupcakes, dip them again. Set aside to let the chocolate ganache set and solidify.

Step 10

Keep leftovers covered at room temperature for up to 3 days.

MAKES 6 PANCAKES

Prep time: 15 minutes

Cook time: 20 minutes

Ingredients:

FOR THE CINNAMON SWIRL

- 5 tablespoons light brown sugar
- 3 tablespoons butter or nondairy alternative, melted
- 2 teaspoons ground cinnamon

FOR THE PANCAKES

- Gluten-free cooking spray
- 125 grams All-Purpose Flour Blend
- 2 tablespoons cane sugar or granulated sugar
- 1½ teaspoons baking powder
- ½ teaspoon salt
- ¼ teaspoon xanthan gum
- ¼ teaspoon baking soda
- ¼ teaspoon ground cinnamon
- ¾ cup whole milk or coconut milk beverage
- 1 large egg
- 2 tablespoons avocado oil or canola oil
- 1 teaspoon vanilla extract

FOR THE GLAZE

- 200 grams powdered sugar
- 2 tablespoons whole milk or coconut milk beverage

- ½ teaspoon vanilla extract

Directions:

TO MAKE THE CINNAMON SWIRL

Step 1

In a small bowl, stir together the brown sugar, melted butter, and cinnamon until blended.

TO MAKE THE PANCAKES

Step 2

Heat a skillet or griddle over medium heat and coat it with cooking spray. (Because these pancakes have the delicate cinnamon swirl, I do not recommend using butter to coat the pan.)

Step 3

In a medium bowl, whisk the flour, sugar, baking powder, salt, xanthan gum, baking soda, and cinnamon to combine. Add the milk, egg, oil, and vanilla and stir to combine. Let the batter sit for 5 minutes.

Step 4

Add the cinnamon swirl to a piping bag or plastic bag. Snip the tip about ¼ inch wide and place the bag in a large glass with the tip bent up so the swirl doesn't spill out.

Step 5

Place ¼ cup of batter for each pancake in the hot skillet. Do not overcrowd the skillet. Pipe a swirl of the cinnamon mixture onto each pancake. Cook for 3 minutes, or until bubbles form and pop. Carefully flip the pancake and cook for 2 to 3 minutes more, or until set, watching closely to avoid burning the cinnamon swirl.

Step 6

Repeat with the remaining batter and cinnamon swirl, wiping the skillet clean between batches if the swirl makes it too sticky, and adding more cooking spray as needed.

TO MAKE THE GLAZE

Step 7

In a small bowl, whisk the powdered sugar, milk, and vanilla until smooth.

Step 8

Drizzle the glaze over each pancake and serve. These are best served warm the same day.

The Infamous Pumpkin Muffins

MAKES 12 MUFFINS

Prep time: 10 minutes

Cook time: 25 minutes

Ingredients:

- 250 grams All-Purpose Flour Blend
- 2 teaspoons baking powder
- 1½ teaspoons ground cinnamon
- 1 teaspoon pumpkin pie spice
- 1 teaspoon xanthan gum
- ½ teaspoon baking soda
- ½ teaspoon salt
- 100 grams light brown sugar
- 2 large eggs
- ½ cup avocado oil or canola oil
- ½ cup maple syrup
- 2 teaspoons vanilla extract
- 225 grams pumpkin puree
- Cane sugar or granulated sugar, for sprinkling (optional)

Directions:

Step 1

Preheat the oven to 425°F. Line a 12-cup muffin tin with cupcake liners.

Step 2

In a medium bowl, whisk the flour, baking powder, cinnamon, pumpkin pie spice, xanthan gum, baking soda, and salt to combine.

Step 3

In another medium bowl, whisk the brown sugar, eggs, oil, maple syrup, and vanilla until smooth.

Step 4

Add the flour mixture to the egg mixture and mix with a rubber spatula until combined. Fold in the pumpkin. Do not overmix. Evenly divide the batter between the prepared muffin cups. Sprinkle the top of each muffin with sugar (if using).

Step 5

Bake for 5 minutes to let the muffins set, then (without opening the oven) reduce the oven temperature to 350°F and bake for 20 minutes more, or until a toothpick inserted into the center of a muffin comes out clean.

Step 6

Let the muffins cool in the pan for 15 minutes, then transfer them to a wire rack. Serve warm or let cool completely. Store leftovers in an airtight container at room temperature for up to 3 days.

Double-Chocolate Chunk Muffins

MAKES 12 MUFFINS

Prep time: 15 minutes

Cook time: 25 minutes

Ingredients:

- 250 grams All-Purpose Flour Blend
- 75 grams Dutch-process cocoa powder
- 2 teaspoons baking powder
- 1 teaspoon xanthan gum
- ½ teaspoon baking soda
- ½ teaspoon salt
- 200 grams cane sugar or granulated sugar
- 100 grams light brown sugar
- 2 large eggs
- 240 grams vanilla Greek yogurt or nondairy alternative
- ½ cup avocado oil or canola oil
- 2 teaspoons vanilla extract
- 270 grams semisweet chocolate chunks or nondairy alternative

Directions:

Step 1

Preheat the oven to 425°F. Line a 12-cup muffin tin with cupcake liners.

Step 2

In a medium bowl, whisk the flour, cocoa powder, baking powder, xanthan gum, baking soda, and salt to combine.

Step 3

In another medium bowl, using a whisk or handheld electric mixer, mix the cane sugar, brown sugar, eggs, yogurt, oil, and vanilla until well combined.

Step 4

Add half the flour mixture to the yogurt mixture, mix on low speed, then add the remaining half of the flour mixture, mixing just until a batter is formed. Do not overmix.

Step 5

Using a spatula, fold in the chocolate chunks. Evenly divide the batter between the prepared muffin cups.

Step 6

Bake for 5 minutes to let the muffins set, then (without opening the oven) reduce the oven temperature to 350°F and bake for 20 minutes more, or until a toothpick inserted into the center of a muffin comes out clean.

Step 7

Let the muffins cool in the pan for 10 minutes, then transfer them to a wire rack to cool completely.

Step 8

Keep the muffins covered for about 3 days at room temperature, or refrigerate for up to 5 days.

Lemon Crème Brûlée Pie

MAKES 1 (9-INCH) PIE
Prep time: 25 minutes
 Cook time: 45 minutes

FOR THE CRUST

Shortening, for preparing the pie plate

Homemade Graham Crackers

67 grams cane sugar or granulated sugar

8 tablespoons (1 stick) butter or nondairy alternative, melted

FOR THE FILLING

125 grams All-Purpose Flour Blend

½ teaspoon xanthan gum

3 tablespoons cane sugar or granulated sugar, divided

1 (14-ounce) can sweetened condensed whole milk or sweetened condensed coconut milk

6 large egg yolks

2 tablespoons whole milk or coconut milk beverage

2 tablespoons grated lemon zest (about 2 lemons)

⅓ cup fresh lemon juice (about 2 lemons)

Directions:

TO MAKE THE CRUST

Step 1

Preheat the oven to 350°F. Grease a 9-inch pie plate with shortening.

Step 2

Make the full recipe of graham crackers and save half for another use. You only need half the crackers to make the crumbs here. In a food processor, pulse the graham crackers into crumbs. Weigh out 210 grams of crumbs and place them in a large bowl. Add the sugar and melted butter and stir until the crumbs are well coated. Transfer the coated crumbs to the pie plate and press them into a thin layer along the bottom and up the sides as high as they will go, working from the middle of the pan toward the edges.

Step 3

Place a piece of parchment paper over the crust and, using the back of a spoon or bottom of a glass, press the crumbs firmly into the pie plate.

Step 4

Remove the parchment and bake for 10 minutes.

Step 5

Let the crust cool as you prepare the filling.

TO MAKE THE FILLING

Step 6

In a small bowl, whisk the flour, xanthan gum, and 1 tablespoon of sugar to combine.

Step 7

In a large bowl, whisk the condensed milk, egg yolks, and whole milk until smooth and creamy. Add the lemon zest and lemon juice and whisk until smooth. Add the flour mixture and continue to whisk until a smooth batter forms. Set aside for 3 minutes to thicken.

Step 8

Pour as much filling as possible into the crust without overfilling it. There will be some left over.

Step 9

Carefully transfer the pie to the oven and bake for 25 to 30 minutes, or until the center is set and doesn't jiggle.

Step 10

Let the pie cool to room temperature, then refrigerate.

Step 11

When ready to serve, preheat the broiler.

Step 12

Sprinkle the pie with the remaining 2 tablespoons of sugar.

Step 13

Broil for about 5 minutes, or until the sugar melts and the edges begin to brown, watching carefully to prevent burning.

Step 14

Cool for 1 to 2 minutes before serving. Refrigerate leftovers, covered, for up to 2 days.

Éclair Pie

MAKES 1 (9-INCH) PIE

Prep time: 20 minutes
 Cook time: 8 minutes, plus 1 hour to chill

Ingredients:

FOR THE CRUST

- Shortening, for preparing the pan

- 1 single Perfect Piecrust

FOR THE FILLING

- 1 (8-ounce) package cream cheese or nondairy alternative
- 3 egg yolks, beaten
- 1 teaspoon vanilla extract

- 32 grams All-Purpose Flour Blend

- ¼ teaspoon xanthan gum
- ¼ teaspoon salt
- 1¾ cups heavy cream or 1 (14-ounce) can coconut cream
- 200 grams cane sugar or granulated sugar
- 1 (8-ounce) container whipped topping
- ½ cup chocolate chips or nondairy alternative, melted

Directions:

TO MAKE THE CRUST

Step 1

Preheat the oven to 400°F. Grease a 9-inch pie plate with shortening.

Step 2

Roll out and fit the pie dough into the pie plate as directed. Line the piecrust with parchment paper and fill the bottom with dried beans or pie weights.

Step 3

Blind bake the crust for about 15 minutes, or until the edges are golden. Remove from the oven and remove the lining and weights. Prick holes all over the bottom of the crust with a fork. Return to the oven for 10 to 12 minutes, until the crust begins to brown. Let the crust cool completely as you prepare the filling.

TO MAKE THE FILLING

Step 4

In a large bowl, using an electric mixer on medium speed, beat the cream cheese until smooth and creamy. Set aside.

Step 5

In a small bowl, whisk the egg yolks and vanilla to combine. In a separate small bowl, whisk together the flour, xanthan gum, and salt.

Step 6

In a medium saucepan, whisk together the cream and sugar over medium heat. Bring it to a boil, whisking occasionally, for about 2 minutes, then remove from the heat.

Step 7

Whisk the flour mixture into the egg mixture. Then, whisking constantly, use a ladle to slowly add a small and steady stream of the warm cream mixture to the flour/egg mixture. Keep whisking so the egg yolks do not scramble. Repeat with one more ladle of cream mixture.

Step 8

Add the egg mixture back to the saucepan and set over medium heat. Stir occasionally, until just a few bubbles begin to appear. Do not bring it to a full boil. Remove it from the heat again.

Step 9

Slowly add one ladle full of the egg mixture to the bowl of cream cheese and, using the electric mixer, mix on low speed. Adding the egg mixture too fast will cause the cream cheese to clump, so take your time. Once it is fully mixed in and creamy, repeat with another ladle of egg mixture. Then add the remaining mixture to form the pudding completely.

Step 10

Pour the filling into the baked piecrust and cover it tightly with plastic (the plastic should be touching the filling). Chill the pie for at least 3 hours or overnight for best results.

Step 11

<u>Top the pie with a layer of whipped topping and drizzle the melted chocolate all over the top. Serve cold. Refrigerate leftovers, covered, for up to 3 days.</u>